*Labeling
deviant
behavior*

LABELING

DEVIANT

BEHAVIOR

Its sociological implications

EDWIN M. SCHUR
New York University

Harper & Row, Publishers

NEW YORK   EVANSTON   SAN FRANCISCO   LONDON

LABELING DEVIANT BEHAVIOR
Its sociological implications

Copyright © 1971 by
Edwin M. Schur

Printed in the United States of America. All rights reserved. No part of this book may be used or reproduced in any manner whatsoever without written permission except in the case of brief quotations embodied in critical articles and reviews. For information address Harper & Row, Publishers, Inc., 49 East 33rd Street, New York, N. Y. 10016.

Standard Book Number:
06-045812-7

LIBRARY OF CONGRESS CATALOG CARD NUMBER: 75-168359

*To friends who helped me
through a rough summer—
with gratitude and affection*

Contents

Preface

In recent years the labeling approach to deviance and social control has generated a considerable flurry of excitement. It has by some been touted as a kind of "new wave" in sociology, and yet at the same time it has been strongly condemned by various critics—who have stressed that deviance is deviance, regardless of "the eye of the beholder." Perhaps by now the controversy has subsided sufficiently to permit a calm and reasoned assessment of this approach: what it does and does not assert; its actual and potential contributions; its limitations; and how it fits in with other major approaches to the analysis of deviance and control. As the pages that follow make clear, I am convinced that the labeling perspective is neither as new and distinctive as some of its proponents claim, nor as narrow and alarming as some critics contend. On the contrary, it is strongly grounded in traditional and well-accepted sociological and social psychological formulations, and therefore its reasonable applications are not only uncontroversial but also quite essential to a broadly-based understanding of the phenomena of deviance. I hope that this study will help to place labeling in proper perspective, and to facilitate the sensible use of this orientation in sociological analysis.

In preparing this work I have benefited greatly from the comments and criticisms various scholars provided in response to earlier efforts of mine to develop some of the ideas upon which I have expanded here. At one time or another, the following were especially helpful in this regard: Rodolfo Alvarez, Howard S. Becker, Aaron Cicourel, Lewis A. Coser, Mary Jane Cramer, Jack Gibbs, Edwin Lemert, Alan Orenstein, Clarice Stoll, Norman Storer, and Stanton Wheeler. Needless to say, none of them bears any responsibility for the final product. I would like also to thank James Clark, Luther Wilson, and Jenny Lawrence of Harper & Row for their interest in and helpful attention to the manuscript, and Adele Parrella for her able secretarial assistance.

EDWIN M. SCHUR

*Labeling
deviant
behavior*

one

Introduction

I was forced to be deceitful, living one life during my working hours and another when I was free. I had two sets of friends; almost, one might say, two faces. At the back of my mind there was always a nagging fear that my two worlds might suddenly collide; that somebody who knew about me would meet somebody who did not know, and that disaster would ensue. I was quite clear about what I meant by "disaster." I did not want to be exposed as a homosexual, not only because exposure might lead to prosecution and imprisonment, but because I knew that it would cause the greatest humiliation to my family.
　　　　　　　　　　　　　　—Peter Wildeblood, *Against the Law*

It's amazing! They don't become any less junkies, at all, for being in the place [the U.S. Public Health Service hospital at Lexington, Kentucky]. All is junk, and that's all, you know; that's the way it is. This identification of yourself as a junkie. After the first six, eight months that I was making it, I never said, "Well, I'm a junkie," as an excuse or anything. But now I say it constantly. I always refer to myself as a junkie, even when I'm not hooked or anything. And when you're introduced to somebody for the first time, the first thing you find out is whether he's a junkie or not. It's like belonging to some fantastic lodge, you know, but the initiation ceremony is a lot rougher.
　　　　　　　　　　　　　　—*The Fantastic Lodge: Autobiography of a Girl Drug Addict*, Helen MacGill Hughes (ed.)

THE two quotations heading this chapter serve to highlight some of the processes that are of special interest when we adopt a "labeling approach" to problems of deviant behavior and social control. Such an approach—which emphasizes societal reactions to deviation—is becoming increasingly central to sociological research and analysis of deviance. Sociologists have long recognized that such designations as "normal" and "abnormal," "conforming" and "deviant," are by and large relative to specific time periods, cultures, and subcultures. They have noted, for example, that what formally constitutes a "crime" depends upon legislatures. What is a crime in one jurisdiction may therefore not be a crime in another, and similarly legislative change within any jurisdiction produces changes in the definitions of crimes over time. It was also explicit in much early sociology—indeed it is in a sense a central tenet of the sociological approach generally—that the ways that a person behaves and feels about himself and his behavior depend significantly upon how others respond to him.

Yet, despite these basic understandings, until recently much sociological research on crime, mental illness, and other deviations seems to have been grounded on rather different premises: that "deviance" is not simply a matter of social definition and that to understand it we should focus primarily on the characteristics of the deviating individual (or of his immediate environment), rather than on the processes of response and counterresponse through which behavior takes on social meaning. Currently there is renewed interest in analyzing problems of deviation and control in such a way as to highlight the themes of relativism and social definition. Research and writing by sociologists identified with what has come to be called the "labeling school" stress the ways in which deviance is "created" through processes of social definition and rule-making, through processes of interaction with individuals and organizations, including agents and agencies of social control, that affect the development of deviant self-concepts among individual rule-breakers. Other problems related to deviance may be· unintentionally created as byproducts of society's efforts at "social control."

In part this change in the focus of research may reflect sociologists' greater attention to personal statements by individuals who deviate from dominant norms, which provide more direct indications than do other kinds of "data" of just how such deviators view and feel about their activities and situations. When we read an account, like that by Peter Wildeblood, of what it means to be a homosexual, we can no longer ignore the vital role of social reactions, both informal and formal (including restrictive laws dealing with homosexual behavior), in shaping the self-concepts and actions of such an individual. Many facets of the homosexual's life are significantly influenced by a dominantly heterosexual society's definition of his sexual behavior (and implicitly of him as a person) as immoral, sick, even criminal. Deviators' personal accounts have also clarified a related point, of which sociologists usually have been at least mildly aware—that efforts to "treat" deviators, rather than to "punish" them, may, depending upon the nature of the setting and the "treatment," be highly stigmatizing and may actually reinforce, rather than reduce, deviating behavior and self-concepts. It was only after her experience with an institutional "treatment" program that the drug addict who tells her story in *The Fantastic Lodge* came to view herself as a "junkie."

As we shall see, these social-psychological aspects of deviant identity are not the only features of deviance and control situations highlighted by labeling analysis. On the contrary, the labeling approach, broadly conceived, also focuses on important definitional processes at the organizational and societal levels (in connection with the "processing" of deviators, on one hand, and with the making of formal rules, including laws, on the other). But in all instances the orientation emphasizes one key point: "Deviant" individuals and situations involving deviant behavior result not simply from discrete acts of wrongdoing or departure from norms; they also reflect patterns and processes of social definition.

Various trends in society as a whole and certain developments within the discipline of sociology have combined to bring problems of deviance and the labeling perspective to the forefront. We live, after all, in a period of rapid social change, a period characterized, furthermore, by apparently high levels of interpersonal, intergroup, and international conflict. These facts tend to underscore the importance of deviance-control processes, for, as we shall see, there is an intimate relation between such processes and the phenomena of social conflict and change. Then, too, general trends toward bureaucratization and expanded governmental activity (in both democratic and totalitarian societies) raise crucial questions about the degrees and forms of individual deviation to be permitted and the means of controlling deviation. Finally, in an era that has supposedly long been dominated by an ethos of secular relativism, we are now seeing some very serious reevaluation (particularly, though not exclusively, by young people) of the very nature and bases of morality. All these broad social factors serve to make problems of "deviance" an important topic for our times and to call into question (and to force sociology to confront, as proponents of the labeling approach insist that it must) the very meaning of the term "deviant behavior."

Trends within sociology itself have been moving in approximately the same direction. From the 1930s until very recently deviant behavior and social problems in general were seldom regarded as major concerns of American sociology, despite the fact that such matters had held great interest for an earlier generation of reform-oriented analysts of urban society.[1] True, there has been a great deal of research on crime, race relations, and mental illness, yet major sociological theorists have usually considered this work as tangential to the major task of developing a coherent and unified scheme for understanding the social order. In a period when sociologists were somewhat frantically trying to establish their discipline as a science and to put together the "building blocks" of the social system, emphasis was placed on those structural features that seemed to hold society together. Threats to this supposed integration received only secondary attention. Structural-functional theory, in which deviations from the "common value system" and disruptions of "equilibrium" are viewed as departures from the ordinary, dominated sociology.[2] Sociological approaches to the study of deviation and control may also have been restricted during this period by the related focus on psychodynamic orientations. As Lewis Coser has noted, this focus has tended to produce interpretations in which "the psychological subsumes the structural and hence individual malfunctioning subsumes social conflict."[3]

The current revival of interest in deviation and control has not, however, been abrupt. All along there has been a "minority group" of sociologists who have viewed such matters as central to sociological work. Furthermore, as David Matza's perceptive analysis has recently indicated, the perspectives on deviance that are now gaining ascendance have been evolved through the work of diverse "schools" over a considerable period of time.[4] One of the

[1] Lewis A. Coser, *The Functions of Social Conflict* (New York: Free Press, 1956), pp. 16–20.
[2] For diverse assessments of structural-functional theory, see N. J. Demerath III and Richard A. Peterson, eds., *System, Change, and Conflict* (New York: Free Press, 1967).
[3] Coser, *op. cit.*, p. 20.
[4] David Matza, *Becoming Deviant* (Englewood Cliffs, N.J.: Prentice-Hall, 1969).

main points that we shall develop in later chapters is that the labeling approach is closely tied to—complements more than contradicts—certain traditional sociological orientations to deviance.

We referred earlier to the use of personal accounts as "data" in the analysis of deviance. For many young sociologists who agree with C. Wright Mills' dual condemnation of "grand theory" and "abstracted empiricism,"[5] participant observation (actually long a staple in the sociological toolbox), personal documents, and "letting the data speak for themselves" generally have become increasingly attractive. Although a broadly based labeling analysis proceeds, as we have mentioned, on several different levels, not all of which require use of these particular research methods, it is true that such techniques (closely associated with the perspective of symbolic interactionism, to be discussed shortly) have played a special role in recent developments in the sociology of deviance.

With these comments as background, let us turn now to a systematic review and assessment of the labeling approach. In the pages that follow, we shall attempt to explain (and to illustrate) in some detail just what this approach is, to evaluate actual and potential criticisms, and generally to assess its likely contributions and its limitations, as well as its relation to other perspectives. Although there has been much talk of its providing a "new deviance analysis," we shall see that in fact it is firmly grounded in well-established sociological concepts and premises. The belief that labeling analysis is a startlingly new approach (and the associated belief that it sharply contradicts other theoretical approaches in this field) is, as we shall also see, based on an unnecessarily narrow interpretation of labeling. When the broader meaning of labeling is recognized, labeling processes emerge as essential elements in any effort to develop a comprehensive understanding of deviance and social control.

5 C. Wright Mills, *The Sociological Imagination* (New York: Oxford University Press, 1959).

two

A critical

overview

T HE central tenet of the labeling orientation is quite straightforward: Deviance and social control always involve processes of social definition. Howard Becker's comments, widely taken to be the most important recent statement of the position, make this point succinctly:

> . . . *social groups create deviance by making the rules whose infraction constitutes deviance,* and by applying these rules to particular people and labeling them as outsiders. From this point of view, deviance is *not* a quality of the act the person commits, but rather a consequence of the application by others of rules and sanctions to an "offender." The deviant is one to whom that label has successfully been applied; deviant behavior is behavior that people so label.[1]

KEY THEMES

Given the important place granted to processes of social definition in sociological analysis (represented, for example, by W. I.

[1] Reprinted with permission of The Macmillan Company from *The Outsiders* by Howard S. Becker. Copyright © 1963 by The Free Press of Glencoe, a Division of The Macmillan Company, 1963, p. 9.

7

Thomas' dictum, "if men define situations as real, they are real in their consequences"—surely a truism among most present-day sociologists), it is remarkable that so much fuss has greeted Becker's remarks. The tendency to consider them unusual and to "argue" about them is largely the result of several misunderstandings, especially of what the labeling school does and does not claim and of its technical standing as a mode of explanation.

At the heart of the labeling approach is an emphasis on *process;* deviance is viewed not as a static entity but rather as a continuously shaped and reshaped *outcome* of dynamic processes of social interaction.[2] It is in this general theme of process, in concentration on deviant roles and the development of deviant self-conceptions, and in use of such concepts as "career" and "commitment" that we see most clearly the indebtedness of labeling analysis to the theoretical perspective of symbolic interactionism. Discussing George H. Mead's theory of the social self, Herbert Blumer has noted that "Mead saw the self as a process and not as a structure." Schemes that seek to explain the self through structure alone, Blumer has pointed out, ignore the reflexive process that Mead recognized as central to social interaction. For Mead, human action could not be viewed simply as a product of determining factors operating upon the individual. Rather, as Blumer has put it, "the human being is seen as an active organism in his own right, facing, dealing with, and acting toward the objects he indicates." Social patterns are believed to reflect a continuous process "of fitting developing lines of conduct to one another."[3] A major implication of this mode of analysis has been succinctly noted by Norman Denzin in his recent reference to "an emergent quality that may not have existed before the parties came together."[4]

2 See Edwin M. Schur, "Reactions to Deviance: A Critical Assessment," *American Journal of Sociology,* 75 (November 1969), 309–322. We have drawn heavily on this earlier paper for several sections of the present chapter.

3 Herbert Blumer, "Sociological Implications of the Thought of George Herbert Mead," in Blumer, ed., *Symbolic Interactionism* (Englewood Cliffs, N.J.: Prentice-Hall, 1969), pp. 62, 65, 66.

4 Norman K. Denzin, "Symbolic Interactionism and Ethnomethodology: A Proposed Synthesis," *American Sociological Review,* 34 (December 1969), 924.

By attending to the "social history" and ramifications of deviant behavior, rather than to the supposed basic "characteristics" of deviating acts or actors (as determined by examination of associations with standard sociological variables), the labeling approach represents a major exception to what Albert Cohen has called the "assumption of discontinuity" in deviance studies. As he has pointed out, until recently "the dominant bias in American sociology has been toward formulating theory in terms of variables that describe initial states, on the one hand, and outcomes, on the other, rather than in terms of processes whereby acts and complex structures of action are built, elaborated, and transformed."[5] The same point has been made perhaps even more directly by Becker, who has emphasized a distinction between simultaneous and sequential models of deviance: ". . . all causes do not operate at the same time, and we need a model which takes into account the fact that patterns of behavior *develop* in orderly sequence."[6]

Yet, though labeling analysis represents something of a break with the rather static statistical comparisons that have tended, despite recognition of severe sampling problems, to dominate research into the "causes" of deviating behavior, it is well to keep in mind that even in the specific study of deviance and control concern with process is not entirely new. It is thus significant that Edwin Sutherland, in his classic definition of criminology, referred to knowledge of "the processes of making laws, of breaking laws, and of reacting toward the breaking of laws." Sutherland saw these processes as constituting "three aspects of a somewhat unified sequence of interactions" and concluded that "this sequence of interactions is the object-matter of criminology."[7] Another classic statement, more explicit in its recognition of the direct impact of labeling processes, was offered by Frank Tannenbaum in his discussion of the role that early stigmatization plays in generating delinquent and criminal careers:

[5] Albert K. Cohen, "The Sociology of the Deviant Act: Anomie Theory and Beyond," *American Sociological Review*, 30 (February 1965), 9.

[6] Becker, *op. cit.*, p. 23.

[7] Edwin H. Sutherland, *Principles of Criminology* (3rd ed.; Philadelphia: Lippincott, 1939), p. 1.

The process of making the criminal, therefore, is a process of tagging, defining, identifying, segregating, describing, emphasizing, making conscious and self-conscious; it becomes a way of stimulating, suggesting, emphasizing, and evoking the very traits that are complained of. . . .

The person becomes the thing he is described as being. Nor does it seem to matter whether the valuation is made by those who would punish or by those who would reform. . . . The harder they work to reform the evil, the greater the evil grows under their hands. The persistent suggestion, with whatever good intentions, works mischief, because it leads to bringing out the bad behavior that it would suppress. The way out is through a refusal to dramatize the evil.[8]

In his more systematic effort at theoretical elaboration Edwin Lemert laid much of the basis for the current labeling approach. In 1951 he wrote:

. . . we start with the idea that persons and groups are differentiated in various ways, some of which result in social penalties, rejection, and segregation. These penalties and segregative reactions of society or the community are dynamic factors which increase, decrease, and condition the form which the initial differentiation or deviation takes. . . .

The deviant person is one whose role, status, function and self-definition are importantly shaped by how much deviation he engages in, by the degree of its social visibility, by the *particular* exposure he has to the societal reaction, and by the nature and strength of the societal reaction.[9]

It is Lemert, furthermore, who developed the distinction between *primary* and *secondary* deviation,[10] a distinction that has been central to the work of recent labeling analysts. We shall shortly explore the problem of defining the term "deviance." At this juncture let us simply stress the importance of always distinguishing,

8 Frank .Tannenbaum, *Crime and the Community* (Boston: Ginn, 1938), pp. 19–20.
9 Edwin M. Lemert, *Social Pathology* (New York: McGraw-Hill, 1951), pp. 22, 23.
10 *Ibid.*, pp. 75–76; see also Lemert, *Human Deviance, Social Problems, and Social Control* (Englewood Cliffs, N.J.: Prentice-Hall, 1967), chap. 3.

for purposes of analysis, between a primary or initial act of deviation, on one hand, and deviant roles, deviant identities, and broad situations involving deviance—as shaped by societal definitions and responses—on the other. As we shall see, some of the misunderstandings underlying certain criticisms of the labeling orientation result from failure to keep such a distinction in mind.

Although we have stated that the labeling approach preeminently involves process, we have made relatively little effort so far to indicate more precisely just which processes. Very generally, as is probably already clear, the labeling school asserts that *deviance outcomes* reflect complex processes of action and reaction, of response and counterresponse. The notion of deviance "outcomes" may be useful, for it encompasses both individual consequences of societal reactions (as represented by the secondary deviant, recently defined by Lemert as "a person whose life and identity are organized around the facts of deviance"[11]) and situational consequences for society at large (for example, the economic consequences of labeling certain forms of deviating behavior as criminal). At times the labeling perspective has seemed to be concerned only with the former type of outcome, that is, with the production of deviant identities or characters in individuals. There is good reason to believe, however, that a considerably broader interpretation of labeling is warranted. We hope to find adequate support for this belief in the material presented in this book. Processes of social definition, or labeling, that contribute to deviance outcomes are actually found on at least three levels of social action, and all three require analysis. Such processes—as they occur on the levels of *collective rule-making, interpersonal reactions,* and *organizational processing*—all constitute important concerns of the labeling school. We shall consider some of these processes in more detail in Chapter Three—focusing especially on *stereotyping, retrospective interpretation,* and *bargaining and negotiation*—which appear to be crucial ingredients in the production of deviance outcomes.

It should be apparent, then, that interest in labeling suggests at least several focal points for research on deviance and control.

11 Lemert, *Human Deviance*, p. 41.

Paradoxically this approach seems both to emphasize the individual deviator (at least his personal and social characteristics), less than did previous approaches and at the same time to focus on him more intensively, seeking the meaning of his behavior to him, the nature of his self-concept as shaped by social reactions, and so on. We shall return to this paradox when we consider issues of responsibility and freedom. To the extent that the individual "offender" remains an object of direct investigation, clearly the dominant, or favored, mode of research has shifted from statistical comparison of "samples" of supposed deviants and non-deviants, aimed at unearthing the differentiating "causal factors," to direct observation, depth interviews, and personal accounts, which can illuminate subjective meanings and total situational contexts.

In line, however, with the implicit argument that "deviant" is in large measure an *ascribed status* (reflecting not only the deviating individual activities but the responses of other people as well), research attention has shifted from the deviator himself to the *reactors*. Kai Erikson has nicely described this shift:

> Deviance is not a property *inherent* in certain forms of behavior; it is a property *conferred upon* these forms by the audiences which directly or indirectly witness them. Sociologically, then, the critical variable is the social *audience* . . . since it is the audience which eventually decides whether or not any given action or actions will become a visible case of deviation.[12]

In this connection, several related but different meanings can be given to the term "audience." Both direct and indirect "audiences" react to either a given deviating individual or a particular deviance problem-situation in a given society. All three levels of analysis mentioned come into play. One "audience" is the society at large, the complex of interwoven groups and interests from which emerge general reactions to (and therefore labelings of) various forms of behavior. Another "audience" comprises those individuals (including significant others) with whom a person has daily interaction and by whom he is constantly "labeled" in numerous ways, posi-

[12] Kai T. Erikson, "Notes on the Sociology of Deviance," *Social Problems,* 9 (Spring 1962), 308.

tive and negative, subtle and not so subtle. A third "audience" includes official and organizational agents of control. They are among the most significant of the direct reactors or labelers, for they implement the broader and more diffuse societal definitions through organized structures and institutionalized procedures. It is on this third audience that the labeling approach has especially focused until now, but, as we shall see, this audience is only one of several important research targets suggested by a labeling orientation.

CRITICISMS AND MISUNDERSTANDINGS

Failure to distinguish adequately between deviance and non-deviance An alleged failure to distinguish adequately between deviance and non-deviance is the source of several related criticisms of the labeling approach. Jack Gibbs[13] has claimed that labeling analysts fail to specify what kind of social reaction and how much social reaction are required before an act or an individual can be considered "deviant." Gibbs is particularly troubled by the "secret" deviant (the undiscovered violator of rules) and the "falsely accused" (who has not violated a rule but is believed to have done so and is reacted to accordingly), both of which categories have been explicitly recognized by Becker.[14] Gibbs has asserted that, if labeling theorists were to be consistent, they

> would have to insist that behavior which is contrary to a norm is not deviant unless it is discovered and there is a particular kind of reaction to it. Thus, if persons engage in adultery but their act is not discovered and reacted to in a certain way (by the members of the social unit), then it is not deviant! Similarly, if a person is erroneously thought to have engaged in a certain type of behavior and is reacted to "harshly" as a consequence, a deviant act has taken place![15]

[13] Jack P. Gibbs, "Conceptions of Deviant Behavior: The Old and the New," *Pacific Sociological Review*, 9 (Spring 1966), 9–14.

[14] Becker, *op. cit.*, pp. 20–21.

[15] Gibbs, *op. cit.*, p. 13.

Gibbs is correct in his charge that no unequivocal basis for distinguishing what is deviant from what is not has been established, yet as labeling's proponents would rightly insist the attempt to make such a clear-cut distinction is misguided. It is a central tenet of the labeling perspective that neither acts nor individuals are "deviant" in the sense of immutable, "objective" reality without reference to processes of social definition. Gibbs is in fact not far off the mark in his allegation that the approach is "relativistic in the extreme,"[16] yet this relativism may be viewed as a major strength, rather than as a weakness. John Kitsuse has properly noted that it is necessary "that the sociologist view as problematic what he generally assumes as given—namely that forms of behavior are *per se* deviant."[17] Actually, it has long been recognized among sociologists that definitions of crime and other deviant behavior are relative, varying according to time and place. Indeed, relativism is central to various classic sociological formulations on problematic behavior, for example, some early comments by Willard Waller: "In spite of all attempts to define social problems objectively and denotatively, value judgments must be brought in somehow, for there is no other way of identifying a condition as a social problem than by passing a value judgment upon it." As Waller concluded, the only common aspect of all social problems is "the fact that someone has passed a value judgment upon them."[18] Empirical evidence tends to support the relativistic stance. It is true that within a given society there may be widespread consensus on negative evaluations of certain forms of behavior, though not necessarily on the intensity and methods of implementing such evaluations. It is also true, as J. L. Simmons has put it, that "almost every conceivable dimension of human behavior is considered deviant from the normative perspective of some existing persons and groups."[19]

16 *Ibid.*, p. 11.
17 John I. Kitsuse, "Societal Reactions to Deviant Behavior: Problems of Theory and Method," *Social Problems,* 9 (Winter 1962), 248.
18 Willard Waller, "Social Problems and the Mores," *American Sociological Review,* 1 (December 1936), 922, 923.
19 J. L. Simmons, "Public Stereotypes of Deviants," *Social Problems,* 13 (Fall 1965), 225; see also Simmons, *Deviants* (Berkeley: Glendessary, 1969).

Similarly, it is unrealistic to expect to be able to neatly categorize individuals as either "deviant" or "non-deviant," with no reference to how they have been perceived and treated. Although some labeling analysts may have been less than fully clear on this point, it seems most acceptable to insist that there is no single point at which an individual "becomes" deviant for once and for all. It is true that we may wish at times to refer to "full-fledged" or "secondary" deviants (as Lemert has described the individual whose self-concept and activities have come to conform substantially to the deviant image that others have of him). And labeling analysts undoubtedly have emphasized the importance of public labeling, especially of "status degradation ceremonies," in fostering development of "deviant identity."[20] Although labeling analysis does also stress an individual's difficulty in "shaking off" a well-developed deviant identity once it has been successfully imputed to him, nothing in this approach denies either the possibility that he may do so or the likelihood of significant (and patterned) variations in individuals' susceptibility and resistance to such labeling. Furthermore, it is well to remember, in connection with the demand that individuals be classified as either deviant or non-deviant, that acts construed as deviant (according to a particular set of standards) always constitute only one segment of an individual's behavior. Commitment to (or involvement in) "deviant" roles is likely to vary greatly among individuals exhibiting similarly deviating behavior and to undergo considerable change over time for any one such individual. It thus seems clear that our characterization of deviating individuals must refer to the set of standards from which they are said to deviate and must always be expressed in terms of degree, variation, and circumstance, rather than in simplistic "either-or" classifications.

Critics have tended to overstate their criticism of the labeling approach with respect to its treatment of both deviating acts and deviating individuals. In neither instance does the labeling analyst deny the reality of deviance, as the critics often seem to suggest

[20] See Harold Garfinkel, "Conditions of Successful Degradation Ceremonies," *American Journal of Sociology,* 61 (March 1956), 420–424; see also Anselm Strauss, "Transformations of Identity," in Arnold M. Rose, ed., *Human Behavior and Social Processes* (Boston: Houghton Mifflin, 1962), pp. 63–85.

that he does. Nobody argues that the behavior that we call "homicide," "mental illness," "homosexuality," and "theft" would not occur if it were not defined as "deviant." Rather, it seems simply meaningless to try to understand and "explain" such deviations without taking into account the fact that in a given social order they are inevitably defined and reacted to in various specific ways. Such reaction processes affect the nature, distribution, social meaning, and implications of the behavior, *whatever* other factors may help to account for the initial acts of such deviation by particular individuals. The focus, then, is on *what is made of an act socially;* this matter is to some extent related to the issue of why individual acts of deviation occur in the first place, but at the same time it transcends such narrow concerns. Similarly, the labeling theorist is clearly aware that acts of deviation, as well as societal reactions to them, are necessary in the production of deviant outcomes. He stresses, however, that the patterns of deviance and control that we find in a given social system are significantly determined by the reciprocal relations between the two. He no longer finds acceptable the "assumption of differentiation"[21] that underlay earlier analysis and that took for granted that some basic "differentness" of the deviating individuals (apart from the mere act of deviating) can fully explain these patterns. He is more interested in the total social context of the behavior and its subjective meaning for the actor (which cannot help but involve direct or indirect, actual or anticipated reactions of others) than in the initial precipitants of the acts.

The critic of labeling often fails to consider the important distinction between "primary deviation" (the sheer act of rule-violation) and "deviance" (in which there has been a secondary elaboration of such rule-violation, in terms of both individual self-concept and behavior, as well as of broader situational ramifications). The critic ignores the fact that social action, as Max Weber correctly emphasized, is not merely externally observable, "objective" behavior; attached to it is a highly significant component of

21 David Matza, *Delinquency and Drift* (New York: Wiley, 1964), chap. 1.

subjective meaning.[22] Appreciation of the subjective meaning (and, for that matter, the total social patterning) of deviation is impossible without attention to processes of societal definition and labeling. The experience of stealing from a neighborhood fruit stand is simply not the same for the boy who is undiscovered as it is for the boy who is caught. The meaning and consequences of an adulterous relationship change when it has been disclosed, even to significant others, let alone to the community. Similarly, a false accusation of wrongdoing can have very serious consequences indeed for the accused individual; that he has not actually engaged in the alleged deviation is not the sole determinant of the situation in which he finds himself and of the meaning it has for him. Nor does "being caught" or formally dealt with (or the opposite) alone shape the subjective meaning of deviating behavior. Mere knowledge of the rule and anticipation of likely reactions can also shape self-concepts and behavior. A homosexual's concealment and self-contempt, the embarassment attending a breach of etiquette as yet unreacted to, and subterfuge by a political deviator who seeks to avoid the likely reactions to open activity are examples. Proponents of the labeling perspective are vitally concerned with explaining such *varieties of deviant experience,* considering a qualitative understanding of them as more meaningful sociologically than mere counting and classifying of deviating acts and individuals.

Narrow focus   There are several alternative forms of the criticism that the focus of the labeling approach is too narrow. According to one version, labeling analysts are so preoccupied with the social psychology of deviant identity and with the impact of labeling upon the individual deviator that they unwisely neglect structural and systemic "causes" of deviance. This criticism is essentially the one that Gibbs had in mind when he claimed that the labeling approach does not explain variations in the incidence of deviating acts in different populations. He went on to ask:

22 Max Weber, *The Theory of Social and Economic Organization,* trans. by A. M. Henderson and Talcott Parsons (New York: Oxford University Press, 1947), chap. 1.

. . . are we to conclude that the the incident of a given act is in fact a constant in all populations and that the only difference is in the quality of reactions to the act? Specifically, given two populations with the same kind of reaction to a particular act, can the new perspective explain why the incidence of the act is greater in one population than in the other? Not at all! On the contrary, even if two populations have the same legal and social definition of armed robbery and even if instances of the crime are reacted to in exactly the same way, it is still possible for the armed robbery rate to be much higher in one population than in the other.[23]

Although it could be argued that reactions never occur "in exactly the same way" in differing social contexts, nevertheless it is undoubtedly true that labeling analysts are less concerned with rates of deviation (which have, of course, been a major preoccupation of traditional sociological work on deviance). They are likely, as we shall see, to view rates as partly reflecting reaction processes, rather than as merely reflecting underlying "causes" of the deviation. As we shall also discover, however, nothing in the labeling approach is contradictory to or incompatible with approaches that do focus on rates; indeed in some respects labeling and the other approaches complement each other.

Preoccupation with the labeling school's social-psychological focus may also underlie the claim that even on its own terms labeling analysis provides an inadequate explanatory framework. Gibbs has insisted that labeling analysts like Becker have provided no means for explaining "why a given act is considered deviant and/or criminal in some but not all societies . . . a certain kind of reaction may identify behavior as deviant . . . it obviously does not explain why the behavior is deviant."[24] This argument, like the more general complaint that labeling analysis is so intent upon reaction processes that it slights the significance of norms, seems overstated. As has already been mentioned, a broadly conceived labeling approach proceeds simultaneously on several different levels of analysis, including the crucial level of collective rule-making. After all, Becker's comment that "social groups create

23 Gibbs, *op. cit.*, p. 12.
24 *Ibid.*

deviance by making the rules" is every bit as germane as is his stress on deviance as a consequence of the application of such rules to particular individuals. True, the latter aspect has been more thoroughly researched by proponents of labeling, and it must be admitted that we do not yet have a generally accepted and full-fledged systematic theory explaining variations in societal definitions of behavior as deviant. Yet the labeling approach has in fact called attention to the importance of rule-making much more forcibly than has the other sociological approaches to the study of deviance. In Chapter Three we shall consider several labeling-oriented studies that have thrown at least some preliminary light on this matter.

A rather different sort of "narrow focus" objection to labeling analysis is directed at its stress upon the ascribed aspects of deviant status, at its supposed failure to consider deviant motivation adequately. To the extent that proponents of this perspective pay more attention to the consequences of engaging in deviating acts than to the precipitating "causes" of such acts, the charge has some validity. The authors of one recent labeling-oriented anthology have indeed remarked in their introduction that "this book takes relatively little notice of the motivations for deviance, but instead pays closer attention to the sociology of deviance."[25] An ambivalence in the labeling view of the individual deviator as social actor has already been noted. On one hand, the actor is viewed as largely at the mercy of the reaction processes; what they are determines what he is to become. At the same time, the approach incorporates from symbolic interactionism a view of the actor as significantly shaping his own projects and lines of action. We shall return to further consideration of these apparently contradictory strains later in this work.

Failure to explain some deviance   Critics who complain that not all deviance can be explained by labeling are also concentrating unduly on only one of the several levels at which labeling

---

[25] Earl Rubington and Martin S. Weinberg, eds., *Deviance: The Interactionist Perspective* (New York: Macmillan, 1968), p. vi. On the relation between motivational explanations and sociological approaches, see Cohen, *Deviance and Control* (Englewood Cliffs, N.J.: Prentice-Hall, 1966), chap. 4.

processes operate to produce deviant outcomes. In this narrow view, labeling theory involves only the cumulative impact of successive negative reactions (largely public or official ones) in the shaping of individual deviant careers. Certainly this problem has been a major focus of labeling analysts, but again we emphasize that there is a great deal more to a perspective based on broadly conceived societal reactions or social definitions. If we accept rule-making itself as one level at which relevant "labeling" processes occur, then clearly no explanation of any form of deviance can dispense with labeling entirely. Even if we are concerned more narrowly with the social psychology of the deviating individual, some labeling or definition is going to have to be considered for a qualitative understanding of the meaning of the deviant experience to the actor. In most instances we shall find that negative labeling is a prerequisite of the individual's acquisition of those special qualities of behavior and outlook that we usually mean by "deviant career" or "deviant identity." It is true that sometimes there are instances of even prolonged involvement in deviating behavior in which the deviator has not felt the impact of direct or official labeling (as, for example, when his rule-violating has gone unrecognized). Even such hidden or secret deviators, of course, fall prey to certain indirect and subtle definitional influences that are likely to affect their behavior and self-concepts. But the important point is that all behavior takes its meaning from the definitional processes in which it is enmeshed. Comprehensive understanding of any course of deviating action thus always requires appreciation of the definitional context—of the labeling processes in all their variety and likely combinations (formal and informal, intense and subdued, negative and positive).

Often when it is argued that some deviance cannot be explained by labeling, the critics have lost sight of the distinction between primary and secondary deviation and think only of discrete or initial deviating acts of particular sorts. Actually in some instances negative labeling does seem to come close to "causing" initial, or primary, deviation, as when an act of deviation appears to represent a kind of behavioral compliance with the prior expectations of significant others. Labeling analysis does not, however, require that it be possible to specify negative labeling as a necessary condition for any single deviating act. No labeling theorist has advanced such an argument, and it seems in no way necessary for recognition of the vital significance of labeling, in the broad sense of social definitions, of whatever sort, in shaping what we have called the "varieties of deviant experience."

Some specific forms of deviation may, it is true, lend themselves less readily to labeling analysis than do others. It should be clear from the preceding comments that, by and large, types of deviation that tend not to be repeated or to undergo elaboration are difficult to "explain" in labeling terms. A discrete act of homicide, for example, seems to incorporate fewer labeling processes than does long-term addiction to drugs. At the same time, it must be recognized that the social meaning and consequences of even such usually unrepeated acts as homicides are significantly shaped by processes of societal definition in the broadest sense. Social judgments on the conditions under which killing is "justifiable" or "excusable" clearly affect the consequences of homicidal acts and to some extent their occurrence. (The frequent comparison between ordinary homicides and killing in wartime reveals the influence of broad definitional processes.) The value of labeling analysis in explaining a particular form of deviance may be related to the degree of consensus on its social definition. It could be argued that Becker's analysis of drug use, for example, has held up particularly well because, given a lack of social consensus on how such behavior ought to be regarded and dealt with, labeling processes have become pivotal in shaping outcomes. From this point of view borderline forms of deviance seem to be especially good candidates for labeling analysis and those deviations on which widespread consensus exists (homicide, incest, and so on) less promising candidates.

Recently Ira Reiss has attempted to apply the labeling orientation (and several other theoretical perspectives) to consideration of premarital sexual behavior as a type of deviance.[26] Noting the

---

[26] Ira L. Reiss, "Premarital Sex as Deviant Behavior: An Application of Current Approaches to Deviance," *American Sociological Review*, 35 (February 1970), 78–87.

low visibility of sexual activities, Reiss has pointed out that public labeling usually occurs only when pregnancy results; even then such labeling can sometimes be avoided through abortion or mobility. Reiss has asserted that this flexibility makes the labeling approach difficult to apply. This conclusion, however, rests partly on a narrow interpretation of labeling, which considers only direct negative labeling, rather than all diverse societal definitions of and responses to the behavior. Partly, too, it rests on an effort (somewhat misguided, as we shall see in a later chapter) to link labeling analysis and quantification. Thus, Reiss has asserted that

> The real question is *how much* of the sexual behavior of females can be explained in this fashion? . . . the promiscuous female is statistically very much in the minority. Some of these promiscuous females may have been propelled into their behavior by deviant labeling, but the majority of the experienced females report that it was an intimate love relationship that led to their acceptance of premarital coitus.[27]

Although he has recognized the possibility of subtle effects (guilt feelings and the like) of informal labeling—by adults and even within the peer group at times—Reiss has generally applied only a narrow conception of labeling processes. Of increased peer acceptance of premarital sex he comments, "Such group support also tends to weaken the potential effects of other groups' labels and thereby lessens the relevance of labeling theory."

Actually, under a broader conception of labeling and with recognition that the meaning of behavior is derived from a calculus of negative *and positive* definitions and responses, such "counterlabeling" can be viewed as confirming, rather than challenging, the relevance of labeling theory. Indeed, Reiss' reference to "other groups' labels" shows that he has recognized that what the peer group is doing is also labeling. One problem that Reiss has acknowledged at various points in his paper is just how "deviant" we

27 *Ibid.*, p. 81. Italics have been added. For a somewhat similar critique of labeling analysis in the area of mental illness see Walter R. Gove, "Societal Reaction as an Explanation of Mental Illness: An Evaluation," *American Sociological Review*, 35 (October 1970), 873–884.

should consider premarital sex, given current attitudes. Yet his analysis rests largely on the assumption that such behavior is in fact "deviant" (at least as a violation of still dominant adult standards); on that basis he has proceeded to examine the usefulness of various orientations in "explaining" it. This method raises the important issue of whether we can begin from such an assumption, or whether on the other hand the very degree of labeling must somehow be built into the way we define deviance in the first place.

DEFINING DEVIANCE

Very likely a major reason for the confusion and controversy surrounding labeling is its apparent failure to provide a clear-cut definition of deviance that can be easily made operational for research purposes. In the absence of such a definition the critics wonder how the sociologist can make the kinds of comparisons required as a basis for any valid generalization about deviance. In Becker's remark that "deviant behavior is behavior that people so label," precisely what does "so label" mean? Without doubt it is this uncertainty that has led Gibbs to ask what kind of reaction, or how much reaction, is necessary before we can say that deviance is present. Clearly Becker did not mean that people must literally use the term "deviant" for the behavior to be so classified; although everyday use of this term is probably growing, it is hardly yet widespread. Nor does it seem that any kind of negative reaction to any kind of behavior is enough to define such behavior as deviant. Yet, as Becker has correctly stressed, to define deviance solely in terms of rule-violation, as many sociologists have been wont to do, is to risk inadequate attention to the crucial role of the processes of making and applying rules.

In accordance with the broad interpretation of labeling to be developed here, a workable definition of deviance must both encompass a wide range of different types of deviation and control behavior and recognize the contingent, almost fluid, nature of the social processes through which deviant outcomes are "produced." As already mentioned, we should not limit ourselves to instances in which individuals actually feel the weight of formal control procedures. On the other hand, to include in the definition all instances in which formal control *might* have occurred (that is, all rule violations, whether recognized and reacted to or not) seems a bit unwieldy. For our purposes, it would also be inadequate to consider only breaches of formal rules as the basis for deviance; a wider range of behavior should be covered by any meaningful definition. Indeed it is questionable that the notion of rules itself is broad enough to describe deviation. This point is clearest in the instance of physical disability. As we shall see, there are several good reasons for wanting to define deviance to include reactions to certain personal conditions and disabilities, which really involve no rule violation (except perhaps the extremely nebulous "rule" that one should not be disabled). From this point of view, reference to departures from expectations may be more useful than is reference to violations of rules.

We therefore suggest the following working definition of deviance (the most crucial phrases are italicized): Human behavior is deviant *to the extent that* it comes to be viewed as involving a *personally discreditable* departure from a group's normative expectations, *and* it *elicits* interpersonal or collective reactions that serve to "isolate," "treat," "correct," or "punish" *individuals* engaged in such behavior. This formulation seems to meet most of the requirements that we have just stated. Its scope encompasses quite diverse types of departures from normative expectations, from violations of formal laws to deviations from patterned expectations in extremely informal situations and interpersonal encounters, that *may* qualify as deviant, *to the extent that* the specified definitions and reactions occur. Furthermore, it is the degree to which such definitions and responses *are* elicited, rather than the formal possibility that they could be, that determines the "extent of deviantness" (a conception in sharp contrast to that of the "presence or absence of deviance," which underlies much traditional research in this area). A normative breach that could be but is not condemned or punished under existing formal rules is clearly *less deviant* than it would be if negative sanctions were actually applied. The stipulation that the normative departure must be *personally* discreditable reflects the view that "violations" that do not reflect unfavorably on the individual's overall identity (for example, some forms of "approved deviance" in organizational settings) are less deviant than are those that do. Similarly, in the absence of the indicated types of response, mere statistical departures from norms do not reflect substantial degrees of deviantness.

Finally, the kinds of reaction involved in attaching the quality of deviantness to behavior are attempts to "deal with" deviating individuals. Particular individuals who exhibit certain behavior or conditions are those about whom "something should be done" (even if only indirectly, as when "rehabilitation of the community" is favored as a way of dealing with individual criminality). This stipulation allows us to distinguish (at least partly) between reactions that breed deviantness and the somewhat similar stigmatizing reactions directed primarily against groups or social categories. The most obvious example of the latter is "minority groups." Although the line between individual deviance, on one hand, and collective behavior and group conflict, on the other, is often extremely hazy (and one may sometimes be the forerunner of the other), for our purposes it hardly seems useful to consider all minority-group members "deviant."

The difficulties in using this kind of contingent, or qualified, definition for quantitative purposes are obvious. Rather than providing a means of neatly separating acts or individuals into two clear-cut categories—deviant and non-deviant—it highlights the fact that the "deviantness" of an act or an individual is always relative, changeable, a matter of degree, and that the degree depends mainly upon the extent to which the behavior is viewed and responded to in certain ways. It is the perceived methodological limitation of such shifting formulations (which, whether explicitly admitted or not, is clearly necessitated by the labeling approach) that seems especially to irk the most vocal critics of labeling. We shall return to this matter when we consider the relation between labeling and other orientations. Critics may, of course, claim that

the difficulty of labeling analysis in respect to operational definitions casts doubt on its validity. Alternatively, however, we can
stress the limitations of operational definitions in analysis of deviance and control processes. (Nevertheless it should be understood
that operational and quantified research are not entirely ruled out
when deviance is defined in this way. Rather, classifications must
be established on narrower, more specific, bases. It is thus perfectly
legitimate, from a labeling point of view, to establish for some
research purposes a category of "persons admitted to mental hospitals" or a category of "youths who have not appeared before the
juvenile court." But these categories clearly are quite different
from [and, labelists would argue, much more likely to be workable
than] the categories "deviants" and "non-deviants" or even "mentally ill" and "nondelinquent.")

It may well be that "deviance" is most usefully viewed as a
"sensitizing concept" (to adopt Blumer's phrasing), rather than as
a "definitive" (operational) one. Noting that such sensitizing
concepts rest on "a general sense of what is relevant," Blumer has
further remarked:

> A definitive concept refers precisely to what is common to a
> class of objects, by the aid of a clear definition in terms of at-
> tributes or fixed bench marks. This definition, or the bench marks,
> serve as a means of clearly identifying the individual instance of
> the class and the make-up of that instance that is covered by the
> concept. A sensitizing concept lacks such specification of attributes
> or bench marks and consequently it does not enable the user to
> move directly to the instance and its relevant content. Instead, it
> gives the user a general sense of reference and guidance in
> approaching empirical instances.[28]

As Gideon Sjoberg and Roger Nett have recently pointed out, a
preference for sensitizing over operational concepts is consistent
with, and in fact rests upon, a view of the social order that emphasizes fluidity and the ability of the actor to reshape his environment.[29] It should be clear from our earlier comments that

28 Blumer, "What Is Wrong with Social Theory?" in Blumer, *Symbolic Interactionism,* pp. 147–148.
29 Gideon Sjoberg and Roger Nett, *A Methodology for Social Research* (New
York: Harper & Row, 1968), p. 59.

this view, largely associated with the school of symbolic inter-actionism, has significantly shaped the labeling approach to deviance. Even if our working definition of deviance goes a bit farther toward specifying "bench marks" than Blumer's comments seem to prescribe, a general characterization of it as sensitizing, rather than as operational, is probably warranted.

A *preliminary assessment*

To appreciate fully the merits of the labeling approach, we shall have to examine its usefulness in illuminating various specific deviance and control situations and also to explore systematically its relation to other theoretical orientations; both these tasks will be undertaken in the chapters to come. It may, however, be useful—partly in summary and partly to highlight some considerations that should be kept in mind as we pursue our more intensive investigations—to offer a brief preliminary assessment of this orientation.

We have seen that the emphasis on labeling signals a shift from the long-dominant effort to differentiate supposedly "causal" characteristics of offending individuals to intensive exploration of the processes that produce deviant outcomes. We have argued, furthermore, for an extremely broad interpretation of labeling—to cover a number of specific interactional processes at different "levels" in the social system. Although labeling analysts have sometimes tended to focus rather narrowly on the ways in which processes of interpersonal action and reaction culminate in the shaping of individual deviant identity, there is no reason why the labeling perspective must be restricted to this focus (or to this social-psychological level of analysis). In fact, as we shall see, important work generated by the labeling orientation has gone well beyond this particular concern. It may therefore be valuable to keep in mind the term "deviance outcomes," for, as we have already noted, such outcomes are not merely individual. Deviance outcomes at the situational and systemic levels are also partly "produced" by processes of societal definition and reaction.

At all relevant levels of analysis and regardless of the specific aspects of societal reactions under examination, attention to such *reactions*—to what *others* are doing or have done and not simply to what the deviating individual has done—is clearly a hallmark of the labeling approach. Although it has been acknowledged for some time that deviance and control are interrelated and that it is impossible to understand one without an understanding of the other, there has now been an actual shift in research and analytic attention to the *control* side of the interrelation. Previously a surprisingly unsophisticated acceptance of the notion that the deviance aspect must be more important predominated; even sociologists tended to take deviance as a "given," to view social problems as generating societal responses but seldom as reflecting those responses. A few possible reasons for this tendency have already been noted. The shift in attention from deviance to control has been strongly endorsed by Lemert in the preface to a recent collection of his essays. He has noted that the concern with control and its consequences for deviance is

> a large turn away from older sociology which tended to rest heavily upon the idea that deviance leads to social control. I have come to believe that the reverse idea, i.e., social control leads to social deviance, is equally tenable and the potentially richer premise for studying deviance in modern society. . . . [If we accept this premise,] social control must be taken as an independent variable rather than as a constant, or merely reciprocal, societal reaction to deviation.[30]

This emphasis on control has, of course, led to new investigations of the several "audiences" that respond to deviation. It should be stressed again, however, that, despite contrary claims by critics, the deviating act and individual are not left completely out of the picture by "labelists." Indeed, Becker has made this point quite clear: "whether a given act is deviant or not depends in part on the nature of the act (that is, whether or not it violates some rule) and in part on what other people do about it."[31] One

30 Lemert, *Human Deviance*, p. v.
31 Becker, *op. cit.*, p. 14.

who prefers the labeling orientation does not necessarily consider research into the personal and social characteristics of deviating individuals to be totally discredited or useless. On the contrary, as we shall see, such research produces important findings that cannot be seen in terms of labeling alone. In fact, among such findings are those that bear directly upon the issue of patterned differentials in susceptibility and resistance to various kinds of labeling.

In general the labeling approach should not, and indeed cannot be seen in terms of labeling alone. In fact, among such as we shall see in Chapter Six, at least several approaches turn out to be complementary. There is considerable interweaving, we shall find, of concepts and themes drawn from the different approaches, so that certain applications of the "functional" approach, for example, are fully consistent with, even required by, the "labeling" approach. The specification of labeling processes can also provide a picture of the intervening social mechanisms through which the effects of the structural, situational, and social-psychological variables that have been the main concern of traditional deviance analysis are mediated.

In a sense, one of the most important accomplishments of recent labeling analyses has been to recall, codify, organize, and apply in specific research contexts a number of basic sociological understandings about deviance and control that had been previously recognized but not much used in research and analysis. For example, as we have seen, the relativity of deviance has long been recognized by sociologists. Criminologists have frequently pointed out that the changing nature of the criminal law is an indication that categories of crime are not immutable. Yet it has remained for the labeling analysts to recognize more fully the fact that such societal judgments always help to shape the phenomena of deviance—and to make it a focus for research. Similarly, if we had asked earlier sociologists whether individuals tend to be clearly either "deviant" or "non-deviant," most responses would have reflected appreciation of the tremendous variation in the extent to which individual lives are organized around specific acts or types of behavior. Yet much of the research on deviance continued to be conducted as if deviance were an "either-or" characteristic of individuals. The labeling theorist's stress on degrees of "commitment" to deviant roles and on the distinction between deviating acts and deviant identities has helped to render such simplistic conceptions less acceptable. At the same time, labeling analysis has highlighted the very important point that, although deviance "is not like that," people tend in their everyday attitudes and interactions to behave as if it were. This common tendency to categorize (to label definitively and inclusively) those who deviate has been well depicted by Becker; drawing on quite traditional sociological conceptions,[32] he has noted that deviance tends to be a "master status."[33] Our knowledge or assumption of an individual's involvement in deviation overwhelms what other knowledge of him we may have or dampens our desire to obtain such knowledge. Our picture of him is primarily determined by the belief that he has deviated.

Other well-known features of social situations involving deviance that have not often been incorporated into research and analysis and that the labeling orientation has brought to the fore include the conflict or political aspect and the close relation between deviance and social change. As Becker has reminded us:

> In addition to recognizing that deviance is created by the responses of people to particular kinds of behavior, by labeling of that behavior as deviant, we must also keep in mind that the rules created and maintained by such labeling are not universally agreed to. Instead, they are the object of conflict and disagreement, part of the political process of society.[34]

This point should hardly have seemed startling to sociologists, though as we have already seen forces at work in recent American sociology have tended to restrict recognition of the central role of conflict in society. Yet it required a theoretical orientation in which

---

[32] See Everett C. Hughes, "Dilemmas and Contradictions of Status," *American Journal of Sociology*, 50 (March 1945), 353–359.

[33] Becker, *op. cit.*, pp. 31–34.

[34] *Ibid.*, p. 18.

rule-making is a major focal point before the conflict-political features of deviance problems could emerge to prominence. Recently John Lofland has considered this element so crucial as to provide a basis for defining deviance: "Deviance is the name of the conflict game in which individuals or loosely organized small groups with little power are strongly feared by a well-organized, sizable minority or majority who have a large amount of power."[35] This formulation may help to distinguish between deviance situations and other social situations involving conflict, and certainly Lofland is correct in having stressed conflict and power as key elements in shaping deviance outcomes, a point to which we shall return. For our purposes, however, it may be more useful to consider power differentials as significant determinants of susceptibility and resistance to labeling processes than to build such differentials directly into a definition of deviance.

In our consideration of labeling at the "level of collective rule-making," we shall also examine the close relation and often hazy boundary between deviance and social change. We may well conclude that sometimes social change represents individual deviation that has "succeeded" or "become organized and politically effective." (Such a description seems quite appropriate, for example, to drug addicts, homosexuals, and other types of "deviating" individuals who form political action groups and actively "lobby" for changes in the legislation governing their behavior.) Once again recognition that deviance and change are intimately related requires no departure from standard sociological concepts, but the labeling school seems to have been a particularly potent force in emphasizing this relation.

A similar general point can be made in connection with method: The labeling approach does not represent a striking departure from standard, acceptable research methods; rather it has fostered renewed appreciation and use of some basic sociological methods that had fallen into relative professional disrepute. As we have seen, there is renewed interest among American sociologists in the use of participant observation and related techniques. Such

[35] John Lofland, *Deviance and Identity* (Englewood Cliffs, N.J.: Prentice-Hall, 1969), p. 14.

techniques are particularly appropriate to efforts at capturing and depicting the nature and impact of the social processes on which the labeling approach to deviance focuses. What is particularly distinctive about participant observation, as Severyn Bruyn has noted,

> is the manner by which the researcher gains knowledge. By taking the role of his subjects he re-creates in his own imagination and experience the thoughts and feelings which are in the minds of those he studies. It is through a process of symbolic interpretation of the "experienced culture" that the observer works with his data and discovers meanings in them.[36]

Such efforts at deeper understanding have a substantial tradition in the sociology of deviance,[37] yet before the influence of the labeling school this tradition appeared likely to be overwhelmed by preferences for research geared to statistical comparison of "matched samples." Ned Polsky has been led to comment, in an essay highly critical of conventional research in criminology, that the capacity for direct observation has been "trained out" of too many sociologists who "can't see people any more, except through punched cards and one-way mirrors." Polsky has called for direct, free-ranging study of criminal offenders in their "natural settings" and has argued that the inhibitions toward such research rest on the shortsightedness and misgivings of sociologists, rather than on actual, insurmountable obstacles to using such techniques.[38]

A related issue suggested by these comments involves the vantage point from which we view problems of deviation and control. Labeling and related analyses have strongly challenged the notion that the sociologist can explore deviation without selecting some vantage point (other than that of professional "value neutrality"). As Becker has pointed out, traditional deviance analyses have in fact usually taken as a point of departure the definitions

[36] Severyn Bruyn, *The Human Perspective in Sociology* (Englewood Cliffs, N.J.: Prentice-Hall, 1966), p. 12.

[37] See, for example, Becker's introduction to the reissue of Clifford R. Shaw, *The Jack-Roller* (Chicago: Phoenix, 1966).

[38] Ned Polsky, *Hustlers, Beats, and Others* (Chicago: Aldine, 1967), pp. 117–149.

and perspectives of the conformists and controllers. Yet it is important sociologically that, to the socially defined "rule-breaker," those who define and condemn him may appear as deviants, as "outsiders."[39] To the extent that the labeling school has sought understanding of deviant experience from the point of view of the deviating individual, the distinctive qualities of intensive observation noted by Bruyn have become extremely valuable in deviance research.

We should not receive the impression, however, that participant observation is the only research technique relevant to a labeling approach. At least if we accept the broad interpretation of labeling to be set forth here, which includes rule-making as well as the application of rules to specific individuals, the labeling approach calls for more comparative and historical research, and certain techniques developed in organizational analysis may also be extremely useful. Indeed we could very likely select any existing sociological research method and easily find examples of its usefulness in analyzing the labeling aspects of deviance and control; to cite just one example from actual research, content analysis of the mass media has been used to explore public stereotypes of deviation. As already mentioned, even traditional research based on comparison of individual characteristics may find a place within the labeling framework, beside potentially complementing labeling analysis. Thus Kitsuse and Aaron Cirourel, in their interesting discussion of the uses of official statistics (focusing especially on juvenile-delinquency data),[40] have noted that, though such statistics may not be particularly valid indicators of the actual distribution of deviant acts, they may tell us a great deal about the operations of official agencies of social control. Whatever else they may do, official statistics accurately depict organizational outcomes, from the labeling perspective an extremely significant aspect of the "production" of deviance.

Certainly the general methodological thrust of the labeling

[39] Becker, *Outsiders,* pp. 1–2.
[40] Kitsuse and Aaron V. Cicourel, "A Note on the Use of Official Statistics," *Social Problems,* 11 (Fall 1963), 131–139.

approach has been away from insistence on quantifiability. Sociologists' earlier focus was on the research question "Why did A and not B engage in deviation X?" Answers called for statistical comparisons. This question has been supplemented by new ones: "By what processes does the individual come to feel like and act like a deviant?" "How is the rule against behavior X applied?" "Why is behavior X a 'crime'?" New methods have also become appropriate. Acceptance of nonquantitative approaches has gone hand in hand with renewed interest in developing a sociology geared to a general understanding of social phenomena, following Weber's concern for *verstehen*. It was believed that in Weber's terms, sociologists should once again concern themselves more directly with explanations that exhibit "adequacy on the level of meaning," as well as "causal adequacy."[41] Through labeling and related approaches this search for relevant meaning has sometimes led to quite radical critiques of quantification, as illustrated by Jack Douglas' comments about official statistics on suicide (a deviation to which, because of its total and final nature, we might expect the labeling perspective to have only limited relevance):

> . . . sociologists who have used the official statistics on suicide have erred in not recognizing that the imputation of the social category of "suicide" is problematic, not only for the theorists of suicide but for the individuals who must impute this category to concrete cases in fulfillment of their duties as officials. . . .
>
> The imputation of the official category of the "cause of death" is very likely the outcome of a complex interaction process involving the physical scene, the sequence of events, the significant others of the deceased, various officials (such as doctors, police), and public, and the official who must impute the category.[42]

Granted for the moment that nonquantitative techniques are necessary to "get at" the process aspects and meaning contexts of deviation-control situations, the question remains whether or not the labeling approach constitutes a "theory," an adequate causal

41 Weber, *op. cit.*
42 Jack D. Douglas, *The Social Meanings of Suicide* (Princeton: Princeton University Press, 1967), pp. 189, 190.

explanation of deviance. This matter has been of great concern to Gibbs, who has insisted in his critique of labeling that the approach is in fact basically a "conception," rather than a theory in the strict sense of the word. In Chapter Six we shall explore more fully the place of labeling in the development of a systematic deviance-control theory. For the present, it suffices to note that Gibbs' characterization is probably correct; by itself the labeling approach (with its lack of clear-cut definition, failure so far to produce a coherent set of interrelated propositions, testable hypotheses, and so on) ought not, at least at this stage, to be considered a theory in any formal sense. Formal theoretical status, however, should not be the major criterion in assessing its value. As has already been suggested, the merits of the approach lie in a different direction, in its capacity for reviving basic truths that sociologists have unwisely ignored, in its partial reordering of focal points for research, and in its translation of a good many respected yet neglected notions about deviance and control into a research framework. Furthermore, even though there is no "labeling theory" in the formal sense, the contributions of this perspective to the development of a coherent and systematic theoretical framework for understanding deviation and control are substantial.

Occasionally, writers have used the term "paradigm" in connection with the labeling orientation.[43] Although the heavy indebtedness of the labeling school to traditional sociological concepts and approaches seems to argue against it as providing or constituting a new paradigm for deviance research, at the same time its powerful ability to codify, redirect, and organize analysis suggests that the designation is not entirely meaningless. Of basic paradigm change, Thomas Kuhn has written:

> . . . it is a reconstruction of the field from new fundamentals, a reconstruction that changes some of the field's most elementary theoretical generalizations as well as many of its paradigm methods and applications. During the transition period there will

[43] See, for example, Harrison M. Trice and Paul M. Roman, "Delabeling, Relabeling, and Alcoholics Anonymous," *Social Problems*, 17 (Spring 1970), 538–546.

be a large but never complete overlap between the problems that can be solved by the old and by the new paradigm. But there will also be a decisive difference in the modes of solution. When the transition is complete, the profession will have changed its view of the field, its methods, and its goal.[44]

Although by these criteria the labeling approach does not constitute a paradigm, especially as such basic paradigms most likely relate to whole sciences rather than to specific branches, nonetheless it does seem, at least in the limited field of deviance-control analysis, to exhibit some paradigmatic features. Full revelation of its scientific importance probably will require more research and theorizing. An assessment even at this time requires considerably more detailed exploration of its workings than has been attempted so far, an exploration to which we shall now turn.

[44] Thomas S. Kuhn, *The Structure of Scientific Revolutions* (Chicago: Phoenix, 1962), pp. 84–85.

three

Labeling and

its consequences

in interpersonal relations

REGARDLESS of sociological controversy over labeling and the flurry of specific research projects using this orientation, there has been relatively little effort to spell out systematically the strengths and limitations of labeling analysis or to demonstrate the specific ways in which the approach advances our understanding of deviance and control. The very general discussion of labeling in Chapter Two has only indicated what some of its contributions may be. As we have already suggested, there is really little in the labeling approach that is strikingly new from the point of view of sociological theory. At the same time, the potential for partial reordering of research priorities, for renewed attention to some central but neglected sociological concepts, and for general adoption of a new "stance" in addressing problems of deviance and control suggests that the labeling orientation can provide something that other approaches have not adequately provided.

In trying to demonstrate this point more fully, we shall find it helpful to supplement our earlier consideration of very broad themes with a more specific examination of the labeling approach in action. For this purpose, it is useful to think in terms of certain basic response processes and key levels of analysis emphasized by the approach. Table 1 shows the ways in which these basic response processes—stereotyping, retrospective interpretation, and negotiation—operate at the several key levels of analysis. We can view both individual deviant "careers" and more broadly elaborated situations involving deviance as outcomes of these processes operating at the specified "levels" of social interaction. Keeping in mind this intersection of processes and levels, let us look first at the general operation of the basic response processes, with particular attention to the level of interpersonal reactions. Then, in the next chapters, we shall consider some distinctive features of the organizational-processing and collective-rule-making levels.

Traditionally sociologists, in speaking of the distinction between ascribed and achieved statuses, have emphasized that the distinction itself does not carry evaluative connotations. Any social position occupied largely as a consequence of the individual's own actions, however such behavior may be viewed in normative terms —can be described as an achieved status; both a professional thief and a successful lawyer can be included. Indeed, we have probably tended to think of deviance in just this way, as a consequence of what some individual actor *has done*. Yet one of the key themes in labeling analysis has been the inclusion of "deviant" among ascribed statuses; as we have already seen, deviance is viewed as an outcome reflecting what both the deviating actor and others do. Deviant acts alone do not make a deviant; mechanisms of social labeling must also come into play. To understand the meaning of either "deviant identity" or the broader social situations surrounding deviation, we must consider specifically the ways in which the quality of deviantness is imputed to acts and to people.

Stereotyping

Surprisingly, the concept of stereotyping, which has long been important in social psychology, has until recently not often been employed in the analysis of de-

Table 1   Basic processes and key levels of analysis

BASIC RESPONSE PROCESSES	LEVELS OF ANALYSIS			
	COLLECTIVE RULE-MAKING	INTERPERSONAL REACTIONS	ORGANIZATIONAL PROCESSING	OUTCOMES
STEREOTYPING	Public stereotypes of deviants	Reliance on observed or assumed cues (application of cultural stereotypes in interactions)	Typification in processing "normal cases" (classification partly according to stereotypes)	Individual role engulfment in deviant careers
RETROSPECTIVE INTERPRETATION	Rule-making that imputes ancillary qualities to the deviator, as in employment policies toward homosexuals	Consideration of actor as having "been that way all along"; review of past for early "cues"	Use of "case record" or "case history"	Secondary expansion of deviance "problems" of society
NEGOTIATION	Pressure-group conflict over legal and public definitions	Direct bargaining over labels, as in psychiatric diagnosis	Bargaining between client and organization, as in pleading in criminal court	
OUTCOMES	Individual role engulfment in deviant careers; secondary expansion of deviance "problems" of society			

viance and control. The tendency to view deviance as an achieved status may be one reason. Stereotyping has been used mainly to describe reactions to racial and ethnic statuses, which have been viewed as ascribed. Criminologists have presumably suspected that the public has distorted perceptions of "the criminal," and at times researchers have documented the misleading information about offenders disseminated by the mass media. Sociologists studying mental illness and drug addiction, as well as other forms of deviation, have also recognized the tendency for a "mythology" of problematic behavior to develop. Yet mechanisms of stereotyping have somehow never been viewed as central to explanations of deviance. In the labeling approach these mechanisms emerge as a central component of the social processes by means of which deviance is created.

Walter Lippmann's classic description of the "pictures in our minds," which color our everyday interactions, is pertinent to the analysis of reactions to deviation. As Lippmann has wisely noted,

> we do not first see, then define, we define first and then see. . . . We are told about the world before we see it. We imagine most things before we experience them. And those preconceptions, unless education has made us acutely aware, govern deeply the whole process of perception. They mark out certain objects as familiar or strange, emphasizing the difference, so that the slightly familiar is seen as very familiar, and the somewhat strange as sharply alien.[1]

It requires little imagination to grasp that this passage accurately represents at least part of the process by which behavior and individuals are invested with the qualities of differentness, strangeness, threat, and personal stigma that we have in mind when we use the term "deviance."

Reference to stereotyping should not, however, suggest that we are interested here in a purely extraneous process that could be completely eliminated through education. Lippmann himself has recognized that the nature of social interaction in complex

[1] Walter Lippmann, *Public Opinion* (New York: Macmillan, 1922), pp. 81, 90.

heterogeneous societies demands substantial recourse to the categorizing tendency that he has described. Instead of the term "stereotype," we use such concepts as "ideal type" and "typification" (which has been widely adopted by sociologists who draw on the phenomenological tradition); we thus perhaps designate in a less blatantly normative way an essential aspect of social interaction. Indeed, it is this sense that warrants our broad interpretation of labeling, our claim that definition and reaction processes are at the very center of social interaction and that therefore pronounced or subtle, positive or negative, and other kinds of labeling are absolutely pervasive social phenomena.

Again our indebtedness to the tradition of symbolic interactionism is apparent. As Earl Rubington and Martin Weinberg have noted in their call for application of that tradition to the study of deviance, "social typing" is continuous. Just as the individual constantly "types" other people, so he is constantly typed by others and indeed also by himself. Reference to self-typing reminds us that identities, including "deviant" identities, do not always result solely from negative labeling; on the contrary, some people actively seek certain deviant roles and identities. Deviants, as Rubington and Weinberg have pointed out, "are persons who are typed socially in a very special sort of way. They are assigned to certain categories and each category carries with it a stock interpretative accounting for any persons subsumed under its rubric."[2]

Stereotyping, then, both in general and as a feature of deviance and control situations, has dual significance. On one hand, it reflects the needs of participants in complex interactions to order their expectations so that they can predict the actions of others, at least to an extent sufficient for coherent organization of their own behavior. On the other hand, when we think of the selective perception frequently involved in this process, we recognize that the potential for reactions based on inaccurate assessments is substantial. Research into the stereotyping of deviators

[2] Earl Rubington and Martin S. Weinberg, eds., *Deviance: The Interactionist Perspective* (New York: Macmillan, 1968), p. 5.

can therefore serve two important functions. Probably the more important is to help illuminate the basic mechanisms at work in the social construction of deviance. But also useful, particularly from the point of view of public policy, is the capacity of such research to reveal people's specific beliefs and attitudes about particular types of deviation. In the past policy-makers and even social scientists have often been largely ignorant about such matters. Yet, just as meaningful analysis of societal reactions to a particular form of deviation requires such data, so too does any practical effort at assessing or changing public policy.

J. L. Simmons has pursued some interesting preliminary research in this area.[3] When he asked students in his social-problems class to characterize such deviators as homosexuals, beatniks, adulterers, and marihuana smokers, more than two-thirds of the respondents wrote highly stereotyped portraits of each group; these stereotyped descriptions were also extremely similar. At the same time, not all students adopted such stereotypes. On the contrary, Simmons found a dichotomy, one group of respondents displayed highly stereotyped views, the other highly unstereotyped ones. The following two descriptions, of a marihuana smoker and a homosexual respectively, illustrate these divergent response patterns:

> . . . a greasy Puerto Rican boy or the shaky little skid row bum. As for the life led, it is shiftless, unhappy, dog eat dog for survival. I guess marihuana is used as a means of avoiding reality. The pleasure that comes from the drug outweighs the pleasure of life as it really is.
>
> . . .
>
> As far as I know the homosexual is not like anything. They are merely people who have different ideas about sex than I do. They probably lead lives which are normal and are different only in the way they receive sexual gratification. They have no distinguishing characteristics.[4]

A more systematic questionnaire, listing seventy traits extracted by content analysis of these open-ended responses, was

3 J. L. Simmons, *Deviants* (Berkeley: Glendessary, 1969), chap. 3.
4 *Ibid.*, p. 27.

administered to a sample of adults. It was found that for each type of deviation a very small number of traits accounted for most responses, though the particular constellation of traits selected varied with the specific type of deviation. In effect, there was no single stereotype of "deviants"; rather, different ones were attached to particular patterns of deviation. Stereotypes of the various kinds of deviation were highly correlated with one another, however. The tendency to stereotype thus seemed to be a general characteristic of some respondents, rather than a response triggered by particular behavior. As in the first study, it was possible to distinguish between high stereotypers and low stereotypers. The former tended to have less education (though Simmons also found that some of the more educated respondents expressed what may be considered more "sophisticated" stereotypes) and also to score low on a composite liberalism measure that tapped attitudes toward politics, economics, international affairs, sex, divorce, child rearing, and religion.

In a third pilot study Simmons tried to examine the amount of public intolerance (or rejection) of various kinds of deviators. A questionnaire designed to measure the degrees of social distance that respondents would keep between themselves and members of five ethnic groups and thirteen "deviant or semideviant groups" (ranging from homosexuals to intellectuals) was administered to a sample of 280 adults. The most significant finding was a strong association between intolerance toward ethnic minorities and intolerance toward deviating individuals. Simmons has commented:

> This means that the tendency to accept or to discriminate against those who differ seems to be a basic part of a person's way of looking at the world. If a new fringe group comes along next year, people who now reject hippies and Negroes will rail against the newcomers. And those who give the Mexican laborer and the homosexual a fair hearing will look at any new group before they leap to condemn.[5]

[5] *Ibid.*, p. 32.

Average social-distance scores for the various forms of deviation in the third Simmons study were as follows (higher scores indicate increased intolerance on scale of 1 to 7):[6]

intellectuals	2.0
former mental patients	2.9
atheists	3.4
ex-convicts	3.5
gamblers	3.6
beatniks	3.9
alcoholics	4.0
adulterers	4.1
political radicals	4.3
marihuana smokers	4.9
prostitutes	5.0
lesbians	5.2
homosexuals	5.3

These data were gathered in 1965, and, as Simmons has noted, by the time that his book was published in 1969 some of them were very likely out of date. He has suggested, for example, that the homosexual may currently be more readily accepted and the political radical more strongly rejected. We wonder too whether or not marihuana smokers would be as strongly rejected today. At the same time, given the general tendency to express greater tolerance verbally than is exhibited in actual behavior, Simmons was probably correct in his suggestion that his findings should be considered minimum indications of negative feelings toward deviators. Simmons has explored a number of relevant interrelations, finding, not surprisingly, that respondents over forty years old were significantly less tolerant than were younger respondents and that the least-educated respondents desired the greatest social distance from deviators. His general conclusion that "most people don't like deviants very much" is qualified by recognition of the considerable variations in responses in his findings. This range was such, Simmons has insisted, that it would be

6 *Ibid.*, p. 33.

a mistake to speak of "the" public view of any particular kind of deviation, let alone of deviation in general.

Thomas Scheff, in his labeling-oriented analysis of mental illness,[7] has provided another useful discussion of stereotyping. As he has noted stereotyped images of mental disorder are, to some extent at least, learned in early childhood. Even though research on this topic has been spotty, we know that children begin at an early age to pick up common notions of what it means to be or to act "crazy." These stereotypes of insanity, Scheff has argued, are continually (albeit inadvertently) reaffirmed in ordinary social interaction. Even among adults who are familiar with some psychiatric concepts "the traditional stereotypes are not discarded, but continue to exist alongside the medical conceptions, because the stereotypes receive almost continual support from the mass media and in ordinary social discourse."[8]

In a reference to J. C. Nunnally's earlier research on "popular conceptions of mental health,"[9] Scheff has commented on the overwhelming emphasis in the media on the bizarre behavior and appearance of the mentally ill: a tendency to exaggerate and mislead that, surprisingly, showed no signs of diminishing during the period when Nunnally was doing his research, including comparisons of television presentations over time. Nunnally's research was, however, published more than ten years ago. Since then there may well have been significant changes in treatment of mental illness in the mass media. In particular, there has been an increase in "public service" television programs, including documentary presentations of mental-health problems. On the other hand, as such programing has been presented mainly on the educational broadcasting channels, which have relatively small audiences, its impact may have been limited. At any rate, when Nunnally explored, for comparative purposes, the conceptions of mental illness held by a group of mental-health experts and by a sample of

7 Thomas J. Scheff, *Being Mentally Ill* (Chicago: Aldine, 1966).
8 *Ibid.*, pp. 67–68.
9 J. C. Nunnally, Jr., *Popular Conceptions of Mental Health* (New York: Holt, Rinehart & Winston, 1961).

the general public, he found, as we might expect, that the specialists showed the least stereotyping, the mass media reflected the greatest degree of stereotyping, and the views of the general sample fell somewhere between. Scheff has suggested that we can interpret this finding as an indication that

> the conceptions of mental disorder in the public are the resultant of cross-pressure: the opinions of experts, as expressed in mental-health campaigns and "serious" mass media programming, pulling public opinion away from stereotypes, but with the more frequent and visible mass media productions reinforcing the traditional stereotypes.[10]

Scheff and various other analysts of deviance have also commented on the practice of linking, in newspaper accounts, individuals' records of past deviance with incidents in which they are subsequently involved. As an example Scheff has cited the news that "A former mental patient grabbed a policeman's revolver and began shooting at 15 persons in the receiving room of City Hospital No. 2 Thursday." It is significant that such links in the media between previous mental hospitalization and acts of violence are very common, despite the fact that the incidence of violent crimes is lower among former mental patients than in the general population. Scheff has noted that a news item like this one is most improbable: "Mrs. Ralph Jones, an ex-mental patient, was elected president of the Fairview Home and Garden Society at their meeting last Thursday."[11] Such incidents do, of course, occur all the time in the lives of "former mental patients," yet selective references in the media help to disseminate both very distorted conceptions of how former mental patients function in everyday life and the assumption of a significant relationship between previous psychiatric treatment or hospitalization and involvement in acts of violence.

A similar point had been made earlier by criminologists, who had noted the long-standing newspaper practice of placing the

10 Scheff, *op. cit.*, p. 70.
11 *Ibid.*, p. 72.

phrase "a Negro" after the names of black criminal suspects, whereas no such racial designation was included in reports of crimes in which whites were suspected. This particular form of differential news treatment has diminished considerably in recent years. But stereotype-reinforcing accounts of other sorts continue to appear. Repeated references in crime reporting to "an ex-convict" or "a former convict released on parole" have, of course, effects similar to those of references to "former mental patients." They exaggerate the extent to which such individuals are engaged in subsequent serious deviation. The impact of such selective reporting on public policy can, of course, be considerable, producing public clamor for more stringent parole regulations, greater caution in releasing individuals from mental hospitals, and so on.

Often these stereotyped associations persist because they are easily integrated into established ways of thinking about deviance. In particular, they fit well with a tendency to focus on the "differentness" of individuals who deviate; as we saw in Chapter Two, this tendency infected even much earlier sociological research on deviance. Many people seem to draw a certain comfort from the belief that violent acts are committed predominantly by "sick individuals" and perhaps also from the belief that the mentally ill are prone to commit violent acts. Both violence and mental illness can thus be viewed as resulting from the basic "differentness" of particular individuals. As Scheff has stated, "the average citizen resists changes in his concept of insanity—or, if he is in the middle class, his concept of mental disease—because these concepts are functional for maintaining his customary moral and cognitive world."[12] This preference for consistency means that stereotypes not only shape our general attitudes toward deviance, but also vitally affect individuals who face serious imputations of deviant identity.

In a crisis, when the deviance of an individual becomes a public issue, the traditional stereotype of insanity becomes the guiding imagery for action, both for those reacting to the deviant

[12] *Ibid.*, p. 79.

and, at times, for the deviant himself. When societal agents and persons around the deviant react to him uniformly in terms of the traditional stereotypes of insanity, his amorphous and unstructured rule-breaking tends to crystallize in conformity to those expectations, thus becoming similar to the behavior of other deviants classified as mentally ill, and stable over time. The process . . . is completed when the traditional imagery becomes a part of the deviant's orientation for guiding his own behavior.[13]

Such a process is, of course, a frequent mechanism by which deviators come to view themselves as they are viewed by those who react to their behavior and thus, as Lemert has noted, become "secondary deviants."

Another very useful discussion of the labeling implications of stereotypes is provided in Robert Scott's study *The Making of Blind Men*.[14] Before we consider it, however, a brief aside may be necessary to clarify the reasons for including the physically disabled under the rubric of deviance. If the attribution of deviant character rested solely on the matter of blame, on the assignment of personal responsibility, then clearly such inclusion would not be warranted. But, as we are focusing on the *combination* of a personally discreditable departure from expectations and the eliciting of certain stigmatizing reactions (including isolation or avoidance) to the individual, then considering disability as at least potential deviance makes sense. Blind people, partly because so much of social interaction is predicated upon the expectation of sightedness, create feelings of discomfort and avoidance behavior among the sighted and are viewed as a "problem" about which something should be done. Ironically, given the development of an "approved blindness role," those blind people who attempt to conform to expectations for the sighted may become "deviant" from the point of view of widely held expectations for the blind.

At any rate, the experience and treatment of the blind in our society are significantly affected by pervasive stereotyping. In his introduction, Scott has commented that there are widely accepted

13 *Ibid.*, p. 82.
14 Robert A. Scott, *The Making of Blind Men* (New York: Russell Sage, 1969).

attributions to blind people of distinctive personality characteristics that presumably set them apart from ordinary, sighted people. "Helplessness, dependency, melancholy, docility, gravity of
inner thought, aestheticism—these are the things that common-
sense views tell us to expect of the blind."[15] As Scott has correctly
pointed out, various non sequiturs are involved in this statement,
which assumes all kinds of consequences that do not at all follow
necessarily from an inability to see. Furthermore, as he has also
emphasized, these common-sense explanations assume a uniformity of outlook or "adjustment" among the blind that simply
does not exist. On the contrary, the behavior, attitudes, and patterns of adaptation among blind people are actually quite diverse.

Yet Scott has pointed out that, however erroneous the existing
stereotypes about blindness may be, they are quite real sociologically, in the sense that blind people cannot ignore them. Indeed
they are "central contingencies" in a blind man's life. Sighted
people rely on these beliefs in their interactions with the blind.
The stereotypes are expressed

> in the form of expectations by the sighted for the behavior of the
> blind. Because of them, true communications are impossible. Even
> worse, these misconceptions may in time become real patterns of
> behavior. When, for example, sighted people continually insist
> that a blind man is helpless because he is blind, their subsequent
> treatment of him may preclude his even exercising the kinds of
> skills that would enable him to be independent. It is in this sense
> that stereotypic beliefs are self-actualized.[16]

Scott has identified five major types of adaptation by blind
men and women to general stereotypes. The "true believers" come
to concur in the definition of their situation developed by those
with whom they interact. Their self-concepts embody and their
behavior reflects those qualities of personality, or temperament,
that sighted people insist that they must have because they are
blind.

[15] *Ibid.*, p. 4.
[16] *Ibid.*, p. 9.

Other blind people "manage to insulate a part of the self-concept from the assaults made on it by normals." Such a person always confronts the difficulty that his definition of himself is not that which others have of him. In the absence of validation by others, his ability to maintain what he considers an acceptable self-concept is bound to be shaky.

A third adaptation involves deliberately adopting a facade of compliance with the stereotyped expectations for purposes of expediency. Indeed, as Scott has pointed out, every blind person is forced to acquiesce in this manner at certain times:

> . . . several blind people have told me that when they use public transportation, fellow passengers will occasionally put money into their hands. When this occurs, a blind man cannot very well give a public lecture on the truth about blindness; in fact, to do anything but acquiesce and accept the gift will leave him open to charges of ingratitude and bitterness.[17]

Some blind people use acquiescent facades "not for expedience but as a weapon." Blind beggars, who literally exact a price for complying with the expectations of the sighted, fall into this category.

Finally, there are those blind people who seek to preserve their personal identities by resisting stereotyping by "normals." As Scott has made clear, such resistance requires extraordinary commitment and probably special resources of various kinds, and the blind person can rarely avoid creating antagonism in others and some frustration for himself. As we shall see shortly, organizations for the treatment of the blind play a distinct and vital role in "the making of blind men." But this role too is partly a consequence of the prevalent stereotyping, which colors the social situations of the blind at all levels of interaction. Scott has remarked that the inability of blind people to ignore the stereotypes is a major reason "why homogeneity develops in this otherwise heterogeneous group of individuals."[18]

17 *Ibid.*, p. 23.
18 *Ibid.*, p. 24.

As Lippmann has emphasized, no single individual can have more than limited direct contact with the multitude of personal experiences and social situations that characterize a complex society. For this reason alone, stereotyping becomes common and almost necessary. It is certainly true that the opinions on deviance of many "normals" are developed without any direct contact with the deviators; Simmons found this unfamiliarity in a majority of the respondents in his samples. The apparent desire to avoid such direct contact very likely exacerbates this situation; those who conform frequently experience grave discomfort just thinking about various kinds of deviation, let alone confronting them directly. To the extent that this avoidance tendency is present, the likelihood of reliance on stereotypes is heightened, for it offers a relatively comfortable way of dealing with threatening behavior.

From the discussion so far some of the consequences of stereotyping deviance should be apparent. At the level of direct personal interaction it significantly influences the expectations of others, causing serious problems of response and "identity management"[19] for deviators. As the studies by Scheff, Scott, and others have made clear, definitions of the situation held by those reacting to the deviation, definitions that are often shaped primarily by stereotyped beliefs, can indeed have so overwhelming an impact that the deviating individual may find himself unable to sustain any alternative definition of himself. Stereotyping is also elaborated at the levels of public decision-making and organizational processing. Widely held and often stereotypical beliefs about particular forms of deviation frequently influence the substance and implementation of formal legal rules and other "policy" measures. Similarly, as we shall see, organizational practices, particularly the selection and processing of individuals by formal agencies of control, often reflect common public stereotypes or more specific organizational ideologies grounded in stereotyped thinking. Stereotyping can serve at all levels, to instigate or propel

[19] See Erving Goffman, *Stigma* (Englewood Cliffs, N.J.: Prentice-Hall, 1963).

mechanisms of self-fulfilling prophecy, in which the conditions that control measures are aimed at are fostered by those very measures. Also central to stereotyping is the fact that deviance tends to be a "master status." Stereotyping involves a tendency to jump from a single cue or a small number of cues in actual, suspected, or alleged behavior to a more general picture of "the kind of person" with whom one is dealing. This tendency is also involved in another major aspect of labeling, the process of retrospective interpretation, to which we turn next.

Retrospective interpretation

The second, and closely related, facet of the labeling process, retrospective interpretation, involves the mechanisms by which reactors come to view deviators or suspected deviators "in a totally new light." Undoubtedly the most glaring examples are found in such public "status-degradation ceremonies"[20] as the criminal trial. Sociologists have long been aware of the social-psychological processes by which an individual perceived one day as simply John Doe can (as a result of conviction at trial or even of having been held as a suspect) become "a murderer" or "a rapist" the next. Yet again it has remained for scholars using the labeling approach to focus research and analysis directly on this reconstitution of individual character or identity.

Such reassessment of the deviator and the attendant re-"placing" of him socially are not at all limited to public ceremonies. In his interesting research on reactions to deviance, John Kitsuse asked his respondents (mostly students) whether or not they had ever known individuals who had been involved in various specified kinds of deviation and, if so, to trace the circumstances under which they had recognized the deviance, what they had thought of it, and how they had reacted to it. In analyzing the responses related to imputed homosexuality, Kitsuse noted

[20] See Harold Garfinkel, "Conditions of Successful Degradation Ceremonies," *American Journal of Sociology,* 61 (March 1956), 420–424.

a process by which the subject re-interprets the individual's past behavior in the light of the new information concerning his sexual deviance. . . . The subjects indicate that they reviewed their past interactions with the individuals in question, searching for subtle cues and nuances of behavior which might give further evidence of the alleged deviance. This retrospective reading generally provided the subjects with just such evidence to support the conclusion that "this is what was going on all the time."[21]

Kitsuse's research produced similar findings about such other forms of deviation as drug addiction. In those instances too he found that perception of individuals as deviators had usually come first (in the drug cases often through public disclosure) and that *then* the respondents questioned in the study had "recognized" apparent "indicators" of such deviation in earlier behavior.

The ramifications of such rereading of an individual are basic to the way in which the labeling process "creates" deviants. Harold Garfinkel's early statement remains the most succinct and forcible description of what is involved:

> The work of the denunciation effects the recasting of the objective character of the perceived other: The other person becomes in the eyes of his condemners literally a different and *new* person. It is not that the new attributes are added to the old "nucleus." He is not changed, he is reconstituted. The former identity, at best, receives the accent of mere appearance . . . the former identity stands as accidental; the new identity is the "basic reality." What he is now is what, "after all," he was all along.[22]

One of the most intriguing and systematic forms of retrospective interpretation of deviance occurs in the organizational processing of deviators and involves the use of the "case record," or "case history." This version is especially apparent of course in psychiatric treatment; theories of mental illness usually come close to *requiring* thoroughgoing scrutiny of each patient's past life. As Erving Goffman has pointed out, the actual function of case records seems to be almost entirely to support current diagnoses,

---

[21] John I. Kitsuse, "Societal Reactions to Deviant Behavior: Problems of Theory and Method," *Social Problems*, 9 (Winter 1962), 253.
[22] Garfinkel, *op. cit.*, pp. 421–422.

to reinforce the formal definition of patients as mentally ill, and to deny their rationalizations and counterassertions. He has commented that the patient's dossier is not regularly used

> to record occasions when the patient showed capacity to cope honorably and effectively with difficult life situations. Nor is the case record typically used to provide a rough average or sampling of his past conduct. One of its purposes is to show the ways in which the patient is sick and the reasons why it was right to commit him and is right currently to keep him committed, and this is done by extracting from his whole life course a list of those incidents that have or might have had "symptomatic" significance.[23]

In discussing the various kinds of items that are brought together in the dossier to produce a picture rather heavily weighted toward discrediting the individual, Goffman has not meant to suggest that the items are collected for ulterior reasons. In fact, most of the information in the case record is probably true, but—a most important point—it is probably also true "that almost anyone's life course could yield up enough denigrating facts to provide grounds for the record's justification of commitment."[24] Basically the case record provides a retrospective rationalization, or substantiation, of the present diagnosis and, according to Goffman, "a new view of the patient's 'essential' character."

In such "biographical reconstructions," John Lofland has argued,

> we see most clearly the social need of Others to render Actors as consistent objects . . . there must be a *special* history that *specially* explains current imputed identity. Relative to deviance, the *present evil* of current character must be related to *past evil* that can be discovered in biography.

From this point of view such professionals as psychologists and psychiatrists often serve as "specialists in biographical reconstruction" (or, as Lofland has phrased it elsewhere, "consistency" or

---

23 Goffman, "The Moral Career of the Mental Patient," in Goffman, *Asylums* (Garden City, N.Y.: Doubleday Anchor, 1961), pp. 155–156; also "The Medical Model and Mental Hospitalization," in *Asylums,* pp. 323–386.
24 Goffman, "The Moral Career of the Mental Patient," p. 159.

"imputational" specialists).[25] This aspect of their role as agents of social control represents, according to Lofland, merely a formalization and elaboration of similar efforts at maintaining consistency through biographical reconstruction that all of us engage in continually in our everyday interactions.

Lofland has explored some of the public ramifications of retrospective interpretation, by analyzing newspaper coverage of two recent and widely publicized crimes.[26] He has noted that early research on Richard Speck, charged with the murder of eight student nurses in Chicago in 1966, had uncovered mostly favorable information about the suspect and had consequently warranted only back-page treatment. It was not until four days after Speck's apprehension that "enough appropriate material was available to credibly present the 'right' biography on the front page." (Lofland has reprinted the front page story from the Detroit *Free Press*, headlined "Richard Speck's Twisted Path" and noting all his past derelictions and character failings.) In the instance of Charles Whitman, who in 1966 shot fourteen people from a tower at the University of Texas, newsmen were hard put to render a consistent biography of a "deviant." Whitman's history—as a boy he had been an Eagle Scout, and later he had served honorably in the American armed forces and had done well in college—was difficult to square with the image of "mad murderer." Some people who knew Whitman had questioned his all-American image, but these doubts were not really convincing enough to warrant front-page banner headlines. Lofland has concluded:

> The problem posed in the effort to reconstruct consistently Whitman's biography possibly explains the later popularity of attributing his acts to an alleged brain tumor. When social and psychological explanations fail, one can always try biological or physiological ones. Regardless of the character of the account, Actor must be accounted for.[27]

[25] John Lofland, *Deviance and Identity* (Englewood Cliffs, N.J.: Prentice-Hall, 1966), pp. 150, 155–158.
[26] *Ibid.*, pp. 150–151.
[27] *Ibid.*, p. 151.

When we come to deal with "role engulfment" as one outcome of negative labeling, we shall see how retrospective interpretation and the very closely related processes of stereotyping and negotiation affect the deviating individual. It should be apparent from the discussion so far, however, that the potential force of retrospective interpretation lies in the attendant social refusal to validate the prior identity that the labeled individual seeks to maintain. Peter Berger has nicely expressed this general point:

> One cannot be human all by oneself and, apparently, one cannot hold on to any particular identity all by oneself. The self-image of the officer as an officer [referring to an earlier example] can be maintained only in a social context in which others are willing to recognize him in this identity. If this recognition is suddenly withdrawn, it usually does not take very long before the self-image collapses.[28]

At the same time individual vulnerability to imputational processes may be highly variable, depending upon situational factors, social position, power resources, and the like.

Negotiation

As imputation of deviant character inevitably incorporates some exercise of power (for some people label others), it is not surprising that various forms of negotiation and bargaining have been found to be a crucial element in labeling. Perhaps the example most widely recognized and commented upon in traditional sociological analyses has been that of "plea bargaining" in the criminal trial.[29] Criminologists have long noted that most criminal convictions are not the results of complete adversary legal proceedings with trials by jury, but

28 Peter L. Berger, *Invitation to Sociology* (Garden City, N.Y.: Doubleday Anchor, 1963), p. 100.
29 Donald J. Newman, "Pleading Guilty for Considerations: A Study of Bargain Justice," *Journal of Criminal Law, Criminology and Police Science,* 46 (March–April 1956), 780–790; see also Jerome Skolnick, *Justice Without Trial* (New York: Wiley, 1966).

involve rather sentencing after guilty pleas have been entered. Most of these pleas are "negotiated." As Donald Newman, a leading student of this process, has noted, the parties to such negotiation may vary. Sometimes there is direct bargaining between the defendant and the prosecutor; at other times, bargaining may be mediated through defense attorneys. We shall return to this topic, with special reference to David Sudnow's study of the place of the public defender in the processing of criminal defendants. In such bargaining there is a variety of specific agreements that may be reached (that is, concessions that may be granted in exchange for pleas of guilty). The agreements include lenience in sentencing (for example, a promise that the defendant will be placed on probation), promises that the prosecution will consolidate multiple charges in such a way as to ensure reduction in sentences, and decisions not to pursue some of the original charges if the defendants plead guilty to the major offenses.[30]

DIRECT BARGAINING

Bargaining of this sort is but one of many possible illustrations of the highly significant informal "underside" of the formal machinery of our legal system. We shall return to further aspects of such informal organizational processes shortly. For the moment we should, however, note at least the extent to which informal processing rests on the discretionary power of particular agents of control. At every stage in the criminal process (from the "selection" by police of those individuals against whom they will proceed to the sentencing of convicted offenders by judges) we find significant degrees of discretion. The exercise of this discretion, typically influenced by stereotyping, by retrospective interpretation, and also by organizational imperatives, vitally affects the "production" of deviant outcomes.

In exchange for promises of lenience, the prosecution in criminal cases is relieved of spending the time and effort needed to prepare for trial; it also avoids the risk of "losing" the cases.

[30] Newman, *op. cit.*

There is, too, a more general benefit from the point of view of the court. Given the tremendous overloading of court calendars, the court system at large (barring great expansion of its facilities) simply could not manage its work if a high proportion of felony arrests were to culminate in full criminal trials. Newman has summed up the situation:

> . . . bargaining appears to be an expedient method of answering numerous problems of the administration of justice. Our criminal procedure is cumbersome. Legal defense is expensive both for the state and the accused. Court calendars are crowded and would not be able to cope with the number of trials which would ensue if all arrestees pleaded not guilty. Furthermore, no conviction is ever a sure thing, no matter how overwhelming the evidence, if the case goes before a jury. Prosecutors, who need convictions to be successful, know this. For these reasons too, the problem of bargaining cannot easily be corrected, if it should be corrected at all. Bargain-justice appears as a natural, expedient outgrowth of deficiencies in the administration of our "trial-by-combat" theory of justice. It is supported by both the attitudes of offenders who see justice as a purely personal thing, how well they fare in sentencing, and by the attitudes of lawyers and court officials who can only "get things done" in this way.[31]

It should be emphasized again that, as is true of all other components of the labeling process, the likelihood that certain individuals will become involved with such mechanisms varies, as do the outcomes of bargaining processes in which they do become involved. Not all defendants find the prospect of "copping a plea" equally attractive. The circumstances in which particular prosecutors find themselves will influence their propensity to engage in such negotiating processes. An appreciation of alternatives to, and probable outcomes of, bargaining—matters critically affected by the parties' access to relevant resources and their relative power positions—obviously will determine whether or not such bargaining is initiated in the first place.

[31] *Ibid.*, p. 790.

OTHER EXAMPLES

In the juvenile court, where formal procedures have, at least in the recent past, been minimized and administrative discretion maximized, it is especially likely that negotiation will occur—even though in a more subtle, less institutionalized form than the plea bargaining of the adult criminal court. Aaron Cicourel has claimed that early studies of delinquency, to the extent that they focused at all on the legal processing of delinquents, failed to recognize the negotiated character of such processing because researchers did not probe beneath the superficial information contained in official statistics and formal written reports, for example, those filed by probation officers.

> When we merely abstract information from official records so that structural comparisons are possible (e.g., broken home, low income, ethnicity, negative social character), the contingencies of unfolding interaction, the typifications (theories of "good" and "bad" juveniles, families, etc.), are excluded from our understanding of how legal or other rules were invoked to justify a particular interpretation and course of action.[32]

From his recording and intensive analysis of interviews between probation officers and juveniles (which lie behind the written reports that other investigators have sometimes examined), Cicourel has concluded that the interaction between the juvenile and the probation officer itself becomes, in a sense, an element of "cause" in the outcome: probation, institutionalization, letting the juvenile off, and so on. He has found that "The physical appearance of the juveniles, their facial expressions, affectual communication, and body motion are all integral features of the action scene" and that such features are simply not revealed by written reports, however extensive other kinds of information in them may be. Only by directly observing the interaction can we appreciate the "hints, direct accusations, moral arguments, denials,

[32] Aaron V. Cicourel, *The Social Organization of Juvenile Justice* (New York: Wiley, 1968), p. 121.

defamation of character, threats, presumed or imputed lying, and the like, that invariably occur in the course of the exchange."[33] One particularly crucial kind of bargaining in this setting involves imputations of "guilt" versus imputations of "disturbance." On this point, Cicourel has reported:

> . . . a juvenile who is "appealing and attractive" and who "wants very much to be liked and relates in a friendly manner to all around her," is a prime candidate for clinical interpretations as opposed to criminal imputations. Finding "problems" in the home is not difficult. . . . The transformation of the juvenile into a sick object permits all concerned to suspend the criminal imputations of her acts, even though the penal code sections are quoted each time the police report theft or burglary.
>
> Having established the juvenile as "sick," the P.O. [probation officer] must sustain this depiction despite activities by the juvenile appearing to contradict this label. But having the label, it is easier to "explain" infractions by reference to aggravating conditions and the necessity of "more treatment."[34]

Generally speaking, Cicourel has found that these interactions—including the elements of bargaining—reflect control agents' need to develop coherent explanations of the behavior that they encounter and to place such behavior in standard categories. The bargaining process, as well as the process of retrospective interpretation, then, reflects the need for consistency that Lofland has emphasized.

Psychiatric diagnosis has also been singled out by labeling analysts as an arena of bargaining and negotiation. Recently Scheff has suggested that in such diagnosis something rather similar to plea bargaining occurs—even though it is pursued on a much less conscious or deliberate basis.[35] He has drawn on the work of an English psychoanalyst, Michael Balint, who has described a process involving "offers and responses" by which doctor

---

33 *Ibid.,* pp. 122, 130.
34 *Ibid.,* p. 132.
35 Scheff, "Negotiating Reality: Notes on Power in the Assessment of Responsibility," *Social Problems,* 16 (Summer 1968), 3–17.

and patient reach agreement on a mutually acceptable diagnosis and who has also written of the doctor's "apostolic function"— suggesting that the doctor has definite ideas as to how patients ought to behave when ill and that he subtly induces (or "converts") each patient to have the kind of illness he considers appropriate to the situation.[36] As Scheff has pointed out, implicit in this notion of "conversion" is the fact that therapist and client have unequal power in determining what eventually may be a shared definition of the situation. The therapist's definition is considerably more influential in determining the outcome,

> principally because he is well trained, secure, and self-confident in his role in the transaction, whereas the client is untutored, anxious, and uncertain about his role. Stated simply, the subject, because of these conditions, is likely to be susceptible to the influence of the interrogator.[37]

Scheff has illustrated the negotiation process by reinterpreting a psychiatric interview, originally published in 1954, in which the patient was a thirty-four-year-old nurse who had initially reported various complaints centering on her husband's behavior.[38] Scheff has claimed that the psychiatrist's early responses in this interview (while the nurse was registering complaints against the husband and her external circumstances) displayed "flatness of intonation," efforts to introduce new topics, and continual reminders to the patient that she had come to a psychiatrist, which Scheff considers "subtle requests for analysis of her own contributions to her difficulties." Eventually the patient told the therapist the sort of thing that, according to Scheff, he wanted to hear—in this instance, that she felt guilty because she had been pregnant by another man when her husband proposed. At that point, according to Scheff,

---

36 Michael Balint, *The Doctor, His Patient, and the Illness* (New York: International Universities Press, 1957).

37 Scheff, "Negotiating Reality," p. 6.

38 Merton Gill, Richard Newman, and F. Redlich, *The Initial Interview in Psychiatric Practice* (New York: International Universities Press, 1954), as discussed by Scheff.

The therapist's tone and manner change abruptly. From being bored, distant, and rejecting, he becomes warm and solicitous. Through a process of offers and responses, the therapist and the patient have, by implication, negotiated a shared definition of the situation —the patient, not the husband, is responsible.[39]

It may be noted that, because the patient had come voluntarily seeking help, to focus on her difficulties was required by the psychiatrist's role and certainly quite proper. At the same time, however, various of her "external complaints" (that her husband was an alcoholic and abused her verbally, that he would not let her go to work so that she was cooped up in the house all day with her two small children, and that he was not a satisfactory sexual companion) could have been taken at face value as sensible reasons for her unhappiness. In an early sociological analysis of paranoia, Lemert noted the complex interaction between an individual's perceptions of what is going on around him and what is in fact going on around him. Arguing against the idea that the paranoid's belief in the existence of a conspiracy against him is only his own symbolic fabrication, Lemert asserted that

> many paranoid persons properly realize that they are being isolated and excluded by concerted interaction, or that they are being manipulated. However, they are at a loss to estimate accurately or realistically the dimensions and form of the coalition arrayed against them.[40]

Scheff's point seems to have been that the "external," or "realistic," factors appeared less interesting, somehow less "acceptable," to the therapist as possible central factors in the disturbance. Clearly such reactions will vary greatly depending upon both the patient and the doctor, but it is especially noteworthy that the doctor does have an effect. He is likely, according to this analysis, to define the patient's situation in terms that fit his own theoretical orientations. As we shall see in Chapter Six, existential psychiatrists

---

[39] Scheff, "Negotiating Reality," p. 10.
[40] Edwin M. Lemert, "Paranoia and the Dynamics of Exclusion," *Sociometry*, 25 (March 1962), 14.

have been especially concerned about this tendency of the therapist to impose his definition of the disturbance, however "scientific" that definition may appear to him, rather than to seek its full meaning for the patient.

A further perspective on this matter has been provided by Scheff, who has noted that the common-sense way of assessing such a diagnosis is to ask how accurate and fair the outcome is: "Both [questions] presuppose that there is an objective state of affairs that is independent of the technique of assessment." Scheff has suggested the possibility that, "independently of the facts of the case, the technique of assessment plays a part in determining the outcome."[41] Thus, in the case under discussion, it could be argued that it is really meaningless to think in terms of the patient or her husband somehow "being" (basically, unquestionably) the "sick" one, without reference to the diagnostic process. On the contrary, definition of a specific individual as "sick" arises through the diagnosis, and therefore any such diagnostic interaction becomes an important setting for at least indirect and subtle negotiation and affords an opportunity for the parties to draw on whatever power and authority they have in the pursuit of desired goals.

Lest we come to view such negotiation as somehow reflecting the distinctive place of psychiatry in modern Western society, we may note an intriguing case study presented by Robert Edgerton and based on his research in four East African tribal societies.[42] Although Edgerton found that the most severe forms of chronic mental disturbance were widely recognized by people in these societies, he also concluded that, for a much wider range of strange and disturbing behavior, the recognition and reaction process was extremely complex. As the consensus on labeling was weak, the reaction process could be viewed as a "social transaction" incorporating important elements of negotiation. Even ex-

41 Scheff, "Negotiating Reality," p. 14.
42 From *Changing Perspectives in Mental Illness* edited by Stanley C. Plog and Robert B. Edgerton, pp. 49–72. Copyright © 1969 by Holt, Rinehart & Winston, Inc. Reprinted by permission of Holt, Rinehart & Winston, Inc.

tremely bizarre behavior, if acute rather than chronic, could activate such bargaining processes.

Edgerton has related the story of a sixteen-year-old boy among the Hehe in Tanzania; he was brought to a native doctor reputed to specialize in mental disorders.

> The boy, who was entirely out of touch with reality, was half-carried and half-restrained by a number of his male relatives. The boy was highly agitated and would not respond to any effort at communication. The doctor had the boy tied to the centerpost of the house, then, by holding the boy's nose, he forced a liquid down his throat. In a short while, the boy was calm and the doctor began his diagnostic routine.[43]

This routine—which Edgerton has described as a dramatic amalgam of divination, prayer, and recourse to "accumulated empirical knowledge"—resulted in a diagnosis of great authority: that the boy was incurably psychotic (*lisaliko*) and that his condition was "probably inherited rather than being caused by witchcraft or the will of god."

Once the relatives, especially the father, had recovered from the shock of this diagnosis a process of protest (and negotiation) began.

> The father expressed his respect for the doctor, but argued that the diagnosis simply could not be correct. After all, he insisted, the boy had been unusually successful in school and had, in fact, been sent away to an expensive school for which very few Hehe boys qualify. He had only recently graduated from this school, and his father and all his relatives were certain that he would now find lucrative employment, perhaps with the government, and bring both fame and wealth to his deserving and long-suffering family. Surely, such a boy could not be psychotic, especially not incurably so, and most obviously not from any inherited defect. The father now appeared triumphant, and, in a voice that oozed conspiracy, he suggested that he had good reason to believe that his own son was in fact bewitched by a man who had long been envious of the boy's success. The father offered to pay the doctor well if he

[43] *Ibid.*, pp. 59–61.

could identify the witch and the malevolent witchcraft being used, could cure the boy, and then punish the witch.[44]

After hearing these protestations, the doctor agreed to reconsider the circumstances "by performing his very powerful witch-finding magic that night." This impressive nocturnal ritual, in turn, led to confirmation of the suspicion of witchcraft and an assertion that the illness was curable because the witch was known and could be punished. "This pronouncement brought great happiness to all the relatives, who promptly pledged certain amounts of money to the doctor." After receiving various medications the next day the boy seemed to recover. Three weeks later, however, he relapsed and once again seemed almost completely out of touch with reality. "Nevertheless, the family continued to seek out the witch and to plan for the fame and wealth that the boy's expected success would bring." When Edgerton spoke to the doctor after the relapse, he was told in confidence that the boy had all along been incurably psychotic.

> He added that the condition was inherited in that clan, and that there was really nothing he could do. He insisted that he changed his diagnosis not because of the money involved, but because it was so important to the family that he do so . . . "it is very important to them that their boy not be psychotic. Do you think I have no heart?"

As Edgerton has properly concluded:

> Here we have had a glimpse of a full-scale negotiation in which the desire of concerned relatives caused a doctor to alter his "definitive" diagnosis. The parents and relatives were determined to resist any label for the boy that would jeopardize his—and thus their—economic future. Although the Hehe doctor rarely changed his diagnoses, in this case he did so despite the fact that he actually never doubted the accuracy of his original label. It is impossible in this context to do more than hint at the complexity of the involvements in this case, but its negotiated character is obvious.[45]

[44] *Ibid.*, p. 60.
[45] *Ibid.*, p. 61.

RELATIVE POWER POSITIONS

As the studies just reviewed suggest, an important contribution of the labeling approach has been to bring the elements of bargaining and power relations—which are, after all, central aspects of all social interaction—directly into the analysis of deviance and social control. Such analysis has been resisted, or at least avoided, precisely because it has been difficult (perhaps even for sociologists) to accept the fact that "definitions" that we have come to view as objective, unarguable, nonnegotiable (for example, "mentally ill" and "criminal") can be manipulated in this way. Yet in relations between actual or suspected deviators and agents of social control—particularly in the latter's efforts to attach negative labels to the former, in both informal and formal interaction—the parties' stocks of relevant resources and their relative capacities to wield or resist power are clearly important in shaping outcomes. Sometimes a special feature of an individual's deviance will itself radically affect the power equation, especially when the deviance results from severe physical disability. As an illustration we may turn once again to the blind, who—as Scott has emphasized—invariably, by virtue of the condition of blindness itself, are placed in a position of social dependence.

In a review of basic analyses of social power and exchange, including the important work of Peter Blau,[46] Scott has noted that, although a wide variety of factors may cause us to enter into relations that seem extrinsically rewarding, the selection of the particular individuals with whom we shall interact tends to be grounded in a broadly conceived quality of social attraction, an anticipation of rewards in the broadest sense. But unequal ability to offer rewards in interaction is common (and is indeed the basis of the sociology of power relations). Such inequality seems almost inevitable in interactions with the blind. As Scott has

---

[46] Peter M. Blau, *Exchange and Power in Social Life* (New York: Wiley, 1964); see also George C. Homans, *Social Behavior* (New York: Harcourt, 1961).

pointed out, others' ability or inability to see significantly influences assessments of their social attractiveness. "Most sighted people will assume that they will have to offer more services to the blind man than the blind man will be able to offer them." In fact, he has noted further that the definition of most interactions between the sighted and the blind as charitable is a clear indication of the extent to which the unequal expectations are culturally recognized. The blind person, then, comes to most social situations as a subordinate in power terms. Furthermore:

> As a rule, none of the alternatives available to subordinates in power relationships are open to him. He cannot forego the service required, since performing important activities of daily life depends on the cooperation of sighted persons. It is unlikely he will turn elsewhere, partly because he cannot always do that on his own and partly because his situation will be unlikely to change greatly if he does. Finally, he cannot very well rely on force to have favors done for him. He is, therefore, backed into a position of compliance.[47]

Yet even his compliance with the wishes of others (a typical last resort for those who cannot provide other rewards as a basis for social exchange) may not be acceptable; as Scott has suggested, this inability to provide rewards is probably one of the reasons why sighted people often try to avoid encounters with the blind completely.

The blind person's subordinate power position has important social consequences for him. It makes the development of long-term associations with sighted people of similar intellectual and social backgrounds much more difficult than it would otherwise be. Even more distressing are the social-psychological effects of always being treated charitably.

> The blind person comes to feel that he is not completely accepted as a mature, responsible person. As a second-class citizen, he must deal with the eroding sense of inadequacy that inevitably accompanies that status. . . . the problem does not stem from the preconceptions others have about blindness; it is an effect of

[47] Scott, *op. cit.*, pp. 35, 36.

introducing the factor of blindness into the equation which describes the mechanics of interpersonal conduct.[48]

This interpretation seems at least partly questionable, however. At least to some extent it is the stereotypes of blindness that cause the sighted to view the blind as of little value in social relations, and this view in turn determines the power equation. The stereotyped beliefs about deviators, on one hand, and deviators' power positions in social relations, on the other, are not entirely separable. On the contrary, in some ways they seem interrelated.

Scott has noted that it is sometimes possible for the blind man to escape the dilemma posed by the power equation that typically characterizes the interactions of the blind and the sighted. Usually, however, he must possess some special quality, trait, or attribute to do so. We shall see that possession of such valued exchange resources also tends to influence the ability of a blind person to resist certain kinds of labeling or role-assignment pressures to which many blind people are subjected by the organizations with which they must deal.

By focusing on the negotiation process labeling analysts bring out the fact that deviance and control outcomes—at least on the societal level—reflect political decisions and actions in the broadest sense. Becker has framed a vital question in deviance research:

> Who can, in fact, force others to accept their rules and what are the causes of their success? This is, of course a question of political and economic power. [At least at the interpersonal level we might add some notion of "social-psychological power."] Here it is enough to note that people are in fact always *forcing* their rules on others, applying them more or less against the will and without the consent of those others.[49]

And he has remarked that in our society the operative, or at least formal, rules tend to be made by older people against younger ones, by whites against blacks, by men against women. We shall

[48] *Ibid.*, p. 37.
[49] Howard S. Becker, *Outsiders* (New York: Free Press, 1964), p. 17.

return to this question when we consider the interrelations between the labeling and other sociological approaches to the study of deviance. At the level of collective rule-making (as when rules become "laws") these relations among gross social categories seem to hold up. These particular classifications may, however, be somewhat less salient in definition processes at the level of interpersonal relations. As we shall see, which factors are most salient probably varies, depending upon the kind of deviance involved and upon certain other characteristics of the individuals.

Role engulfment

One major consequence of the processes through which deviant identity is imputed is the tendency of the deviator to become "caught up in" a deviant role, to find that it has become highly salient in his overall personal identity (or concept of self), that his behavior is increasingly organized "around" the role, and that cultural expectations attached to the role have come to have precedence, or increased salience relative to other expectations, in the organization of his activities and general way of life. Lemert's term "secondary deviance" is intended to label this tendency, but we shall reserve it for use in a more inclusive sense—to cover not only the impact of labeling on the individual's self-concept but also secondary expansion of deviance problems at the situational and societal levels. "Role engulfment" seems a satisfactory term for the social-psychological impact on the individual. It should be viewed not as an alternative to "secondary deviance" but rather as a subconcept denoting one, narrower facet of the secondary expansion of deviation through societal reaction processes.

ACCEPTING DEVIANT IDENTITY

In considering role engulfment, we should keep in mind two major points of reference: how others define the actor and how the

actor defines himself. Very crudely we can say that, as role engulfment increases, there is a tendency for the actor to define himself
as others define him. Yet, as already noted, a person can be "en-
gulfed," at least in a practical sense by a deviant role, despite his
definition of himself as non-deviant. The increasing difficulty of
continuing to view himself as non-deviant, as more and more people treat him more and more of the time as if he were "deviant," is
a central problem. Basically the problem is one of validating
identity, which Berger has posed in the statement that we quoted
in our discussion of retrospective interpretation. Indeed, the notion of role engulfment is implicit in, or integral to, a number
of concepts and processes that we have already considered. Both
stereotyping and retrospective interpretation seem to imply role
engulfment almost by definition. The concept of master status lies
at the heart of role engulfment, for it is the increased salience or
primacy of the deviant role for the individual that is the hallmark
of such engulfment. And deviant roles generally seem to have a
kind of built-in primacy, or master status, relative at least to certain other kinds of roles. It should be noted, though, that we may
also be able to distinguish between particular deviant roles according to the overall likelihood that they will acquire primacy.
Similarly, there may be systematic differences between particular
categories of individuals in the likelihood that deviant roles generally or specific deviant roles will become primary. That is, individuals have socially patterned, or categoric, variations in their
susceptibility and resistance to engulfment in deviant roles generally and in particular deviant roles.

What kinds of events (or what kinds of information acquired
by others) are particularly likely to precipitate or to accelerate
the process of role engulfment? Labeling analysts like Becker
have emphasized rather strongly the event of public identification
and labeling. One difficulty in this emphasis, as well as in that
on formal degradation ceremonies, is the possible suggestion that
role engulfment occurs "all at once." It is true that a criminal trial,
hospitalization for mental illness, or entrance into various other
screening and treatment procedures seems to have special impact.
Life is no longer the same as it was, and the individual inevitably

comes to be viewed in a new light; he can thus hardly help but see himself in new terms. Yet, although such an event can theoretically occur "out of the blue," only rarely does it do so. Ordinarily if we are to understand public definition of a "deviant," we must view it within a context of continuous interaction, involving numerous relevant patterns of action and response and constantly shifting definitions of situations.

In important research on family reactions to mental illness[50] Marian Yarrow and her associates found that the open definition of a family member as mentally ill and direct action based on such a definition are often preceded by a long period of accommodation, during which the individual's disturbing behavior is "normalized"—that is, its pathological nature is denied or otherwise explained away. It is only after a gradual process of redefinition, in which behavior is finally accepted as symptomatic of illness, that such a seemingly abrupt and decisive step as hospitalization occurs. Nor is it true that being "publicly caught and labeled" ends the process of societal reaction to deviation. On the contrary, as Kitsuse's study of responses to homosexuality has shown, such an event is likely to encourage others who interact with the individual to reassess their conceptions of him. Their subsequent relations with him are likely to be altered, in turn, thus adding to the cumulative processes at work. In this connection, we may also recall the "hidden deviant," who is neither publicly caught and labeled nor recognized as a deviator by those with whom he interacts but who nonetheless may well find his self-concept and behavior affected by his knowledge that he could be so labeled and by his awareness of others' views of people "like" himself.

Other interesting research findings have indicated still further the quite diverse sorts of "cues" (information about individuals) that may activate or propel the process of role engulfment. The field study of "legal stigma" by Richard Schwartz and Jerome Skolnick,[51] in which prospective employers at resort hotels were shown

[50] Marian Radke Yarrow *et al.*, "The Psychological Meaning of Mental Illness in the Family," *Journal of Social Issues*, 11 (1955), 12–24.
[51] Richard D. Schwartz and Jerome Skolnick, "Two Studies of Legal Stigma," *Social Problems*, 10 (Fall 1962), 133–142.

employment "dossiers" on job applicants (which included systematically varied information about "criminal records" of varying degrees), has shown that merely being accused of a deviating act can be seriously discrediting, even though the accusation has been "disproved" (as when "acquittal" records were included in the dossiers). Derek Phillips' research on rejection of the mentally ill has disclosed that an individual's effort to seek particular kinds of help in connection with behavior that is troubling him and that others may view as deviant may itself be a discrediting factor.[52] Respondents in Phillips' sample of several hundred adults were shown five cards, each of which contained a description of an individual exhibiting a certain pattern of behavior. The cards were constructed to represent a paranoid schizophrenic, an individual suffering from simple schizophrenia, an anxious and depressed person, a phobic individual with compulsive features, and a "normal" person. These abstracts were presented in systematically varied combinations with information about what source of help the person was using (none, a clergyman, an ordinary physician, a psychiatrist, or a mental hospital). After reading the combined descriptions of behavior and help source, respondents were asked a series of questions comprising a social-distance scale.

Although Phillips found a significant association between the kind of behavior displayed by the individual and the extent to which he was rejected by respondents, he also found that an individual displaying a given type of behavior was rejected least when he sought no help and most when he was hospitalized in a mental institution. Interestingly, when an individual depicted as "normal" was described as having been in a mental hospital, he was rejected more frequently than was a psychotic individual described as not having sought help from a professional or as seeing a clergyman and more frequently than was a depressed neurotic seeing a clergyman. The association between the source of help and rejection was maintained within age groups, socioeconomic-status

52 Derek L. Phillips, "Rejection: A Possible Consequence of Seeking Help for Mental Disorders," *American Sociological Review*, 28 (December 1963), 963–972.

categories, and groups showing different levels of authoritarianism. The basic findings thus did not appear to reflect differences among respondents in any of these factors. Phillips did find that respondents who had had relatives who had sought help for mental disorders deviated from the general rejection pattern; they were likely to reject individuals who did not seek help more than they rejected those who consulted clergymen, ordinary physicians, or psychiatrists. He also found that respondents who did not accept a "norm of self-reliance" were less likely to reject seekers of help than were those who strongly or even mildly professed such a norm.

DEVIANCE DISAVOWAL

A major aspect of role engulfment, to which we have already alluded, is the difficulty that the deviating individual experiences in trying to alter his situation, or to reduce the "engulfment" (at least when the process has reached an advanced stage). The problems involved in efforts at "deviance disavowal" were recognized early by Frank Tannenbaum, whose analysis of the "dramatization of evil" has been cited. As he has noted, once the individual has been stigmatized as a delinquent or criminal, "the community expects him to live up to his reputation, and will not credit him if he does not live up to it."[53] Similarly, recent studies using social-distance scales (for example, Simmons' research on stereotyping and the Phillips study just discussed) suggest that, once one has a "record" of recognized deviation, negative reactions set in; we must assume that these reactions are difficult to overcome. Indeed, treatment personnel and others professionally concerned with the practical problems of former deviators of various kinds have emphasized the extreme difficulties that such individuals face in seeking employment, establishing themselves in non-deviant communities, and generally in trying to lead "normal" lives.

The difficulties of the ex-convict, the former mental patient,

[53] Frank Tannenbaum, *Crime and the Community* (Boston: Ginn, 1938), p. 477.

and the drug addict released from institutional treatment have all been documented at some length. Such people encounter serious problems in convincing significant others that they are "no longer like that." Their success in managing both practical problems and relations with others bears heavily upon their ability to maintain non-deviant conceptions of themselves. As Marsh Ray has observed, the drug addict who has undergone withdrawal treatment and who seeks to remain abstinent "now enters a period which might best be characterized as a 'running struggle' with his problems of social identity." The ex-addict who is successful in this endeavor "relates to new groups of people, participates in their experience, and to some extent begins to evaluate the conduct of his former associates (and perhaps his own when he was an addict) in terms of the values of the new group."[54] As this quotation suggests—and as should be emphasized—it is by no means impossible for particular individuals to "shake off" imputed deviant characters or identities. Furthermore, that individuals can sometimes successfully disavow deviant identities in no way provides an argument against the labeling perspective. Recently Harrison Trice and Paul Roman have suggested that, at the very least, the labeling approach slights possibilities of "delabeling" and "relabeling"—as exemplified by the rather successful efforts of Alcoholics Anonymous.[55] Although it is certainly true that labeling analysts have paid less attention to these processes than to those of negative labeling, it is far from true that the existence of such processes is itself inconsistent or a challenge to the labeling orientation. On the contrary, that success in removing stigma requires such delabeling and relabeling tends to confirm the labeling thesis.

Although disavowal of deviance is, then, not impossible, it is nonetheless difficult and uncertain, and the difficulties are exacerbated by the very widespread belief that changes in character are impossible (for example, "once an addict, always an addict"). The

54 Marsh B. Ray, "The Cycle of Abstinence and Relapse Among Heroin Addicts," *Social Problems,* 9 (Fall 1961), 136.
55 Harrison M. Trice and Paul M. Roman "Delabeling, Relabeling, and Alcoholics Anonymous," *Social Problems,* 17 (Spring 1970), 538–546.

self-fulfilling nature of such beliefs and the attendant interpersonal reactions, including erection of barriers to various practical opportunities, should be obvious. It is worth emphasizing too that, even apart from conscious efforts to reverse negative imputations of deviance, role and identity changes frequently occur in deviating individuals over the course of time. We know that not all those juveniles who are or who might be adjudged "delinquent" go on to become hardened criminal offenders. And even among "hard core" drug addicts, a "maturing out" process, in which drug use appears to be a "stage" that loses its importance for the individual as new life styles and possible courses of action emerge, has been noted.

A related phenomenon involves the various efforts of individuals currently engaged in deviation to insulate themselves from the demoralization and negative self-concepts that often follow from being labeled as deviant. Many of the techniques cited by Goffman in his study of stigma,[56] like the various forms of "information control" aimed at the "management of spoiled identity," illustrate such efforts. In part they are designed to refute the negative imputations that produce deviant identities, though at some point they become primarily devices for learning to "live with" deviant identities that have been pretty much accepted. Similarly, Gresham Sykes and David Matza have perceptively analyzed the "techniques of neutralization" (denial of serious injury, assertion that there is no real "victim," and so on) by which delinquent youths frequently rationalize their offending behavior and maintain positive self-concepts.[57] Youths who engage in homosexual acts for money rely heavily upon similar insulating mechanisms. As Albert Reiss has noted, some very explicit norms govern such encounters, norms that function to define these situations as only transactions and by virtue of which "the peer hustler in the peer-queer relationship develops no conception of himself either as

[56] Goffman, *Stigma*.
[57] Gresham M. Sykes and David Matza, "Techniques of Neutralization: A Theory of Delinquency," *American Sociological Review*, 22 (December 1957), 664–670.

prostitute or as homosexual." Reiss has found that, as long as such a youth conforms to the role expectations built into his activities (for example, maintenance of affective neutrality, emphasis on money as the goal, and restriction to specific sexual acts), his peers do not view him as homosexual, which seems to be the crucial factor influencing his own self-concept.[58]

James Bryan's studies of call girls provide another example of the ways in which neutralizing and justifying mechanisms can be used to preserve deviators' self-respect and resistance to the negative evaluations of others. He found that parts of the "ideology" that trainers sought to instill in the girls during an "apprenticeship" period were discarded as they became less valuable (as, for example, the value of cooperation with fellow call girls declined) but that other themes, like those relating to the "functions" of prostitution, persisted. The potential for disavowal or neutralization of deviance in such themes is apparent from these statements by girls whom Bryan interviewed.

> We girls see, like I guess you call them perverts of some sort, you know, little freaky people and if they didn't have girls to come to like us that are able to handle them and make it a nice thing, there would be so many rapes and . . . nutty people really. . . .
>
> .   .   .
>
> I could say that a prostitute has held more marriages together as part of their profession than any divorce counselor. . . .
>
> .   .   .
>
> I don't regret doing it because I feel I help people. A lot of men that come over to see me don't come for sex. They come over for companionship, someone to talk to . . . a lot of them have problems.[59]

DEVIANT SUBCULTURES

Clearly these statements suggest a close relation between a labeling analysis of deviance (in this instance focusing on efforts to insu-

[58] Albert J. Reiss, Jr., "The Social Integration of Queers and Peers," *Social Problems*, 9 (Fall 1961), 102–120.

[59] James H. Bryan, "Occupational Ideologies and Individual Attitudes of Call Girls," *Social Problems*, 13 (Spring 1966), 443; see also Bryan, "Apprenticeships in Prostitution," *Social Problems*, 12 (Winter 1965), 287–297.

late the self against negative imputations) and a "functional" analysis, an issue to which we shall return in Chapter Six. Some of our discussion also indicates certain links between emphases of the labeling orientation and those of the traditional analysis of deviant subcultures (itself largely influenced by functionalist theory). We can sense from some of these research findings a few of the major functions of deviant subcultures. In varying degrees a given type of deviant subculture (one organized around a specific deviation) usually serves one or both aspects of a dual function. On one hand, involvement in the subculture facilitates access to and immersion in deviant roles that "members" either feel a need for or find pleasurable or desirable. (A good indication that not all deviant roles are undesirable ones into which individuals are pressured is provided by Becker's studies of marihuana users.) On the other hand, the subculture serves, often simultaneously, a kind of "defensive," or "protective," function, shielding individuals from the negative attitudes of outsiders, from the quite practical problems posed by outsiders' reactions (including legal ones), or from both.

Another set of related functions involves enhancement of in-group solidarity and measures for at least informal social control within the group itself. In connection with group solidarity and the morale of individual deviators, Goffman has discussed the support provided by being with one's own "kind" or with others who are "wise" to the deviation, and has analyzed the functions of "back places" where the deviator can relax and let down his guard.[60] Weinberg's studies of nudist camps[61]—in which a response often regarded as almost instinctual, that is, the sexual provocation inherent in nudity, can be controlled through socialization to a generally unfamiliar set of norms—demonstrate the provision of internal social control. The need to control behavior within a group, particularly when it has important bearing on outsiders' views of

[60] Goffman, *Stigma.*
[61] Weinberg, "Sexual Modesty and the Nudist Camp," *Social Problems,* 12 (Winter 1965), 311–318; see also Weinberg, "Becoming a Nudist," *Psychiatry,* 29 (February 1966).

the group, may be a factor in the content of some deviant sub-cultures. Another facet of the operations of subcultures is apparent in instances of political deviation or esoteric cults, in which complex and unusual belief systems are central to the patterns of deviation; the very survival of those patterns may depend heavily upon the kinds of support that the subcultures can provide.[62]

Most of these comments pertain primarily to what we have called the "positive" or "facilitative" aspect of subculture. But we can rather easily find various examples of defensive subcultural elaboration and involvement. Becker has shown how learning the norms of marihuana use (and the close association with other users required) helps the user to deal with the problems of supply, secrecy, and societal definition to which his behavior gives rise. Similarly, many of the subcultural features surrounding heroin addiction serve an even more direct defensive function, permitting the addict to deal with the substantial and very serious enforcement efforts designed to block his access to drugs and to identify and isolate him.

Almost always we find combinations of these diverse functions. For example, the homosexual subculture clearly facilitates the deviator's relaxed association with others of his own kind; yet to some extent it also provides a kind of protective segregation from police harassment and other interference by the "straight" world. In an interesting analysis of "bottle gangs" (groups of indigent street drinkers created for the purpose of purchasing and sharing bottles of liquor), Rubington has noted internal control functions (making sure that the members making the purchases do return with the bottles), general facilitative functions (shaping a pleasant cooperative experience, and helping to order the members' daily round), and defensive functions (shielding participants from police scrutiny).[63]

Although immersion in a deviant subculture may be one

---

[62] Simmons, "Maintaining Deviant Belief Systems: A Case Study," *Social Problems*, 11 (Winter 1964), 250–256.
[63] Rubington, "Variations in Bottle-Gang Controls," in Rubington and Weinberg, *op. cit.*, pp. 303–316.

prime indicator of role engulfment, it does not at all follow that such immersion is a necessary condition of the individual's developing a strong deviant self-concept. As we have noted elsewhere, whether or not a given kind of deviation gives rise to a special subculture depends in part upon "the need for continuous contact with other like individuals in order for the basic deviant acts to be carried out."[64] But, even without such a need, the deviating individual often experiences role engulfment when he confronts strong negative social reactions, whatever form they may take. The crucial point has been highlighted in Lemert's classic statement:

> When a person begins to employ his deviant behavior or a role based upon it as a means of defense, attack, or adjustment to the overt and covert problems created by the consequent societal reaction to him, his deviation is secondary.[65]

It is not the particular form of deviation or the specific content of the societal reaction that determines role engulfment so much as simply that there is a sufficient "progressive reciprocal relationship" between the two. As Lemert has further remarked, the development of secondary deviation usually involves a sequence of interaction along these approximate lines:

> . . . (1) primary deviation; (2) social penalties; (3) further primary deviation; (4) stronger penalties and rejections; (5) further deviation, perhaps with hostilities and resentment beginning to focus upon those doing the penalizing; (6) crisis reached in the tolerance quotient, expressed in formal action by the community stigmatizing the deviant; (7) strengthening of the deviant conduct as a reaction to the stigmatizing and penalties; (8) ultimate acceptance of deviant social status and efforts at adjustment on the basis of the associated role.[66]

The "content" of those actions and reactions and the point reached on the continuum, ranging from initial acts of deviation, to full elaboration of patterns of secondary deviance, will be highly vari-

---

[64] Edwin M. Schur, *Crimes Without Victims* (Englewood Cliffs, N.J.: Prentice-Hall, 1965), pp. 172–173.
[65] Lemert, *Social Pathology* (New York: McGraw-Hill, 1951), p. 76.
[66] *Ibid.*, p. 77.

able, according to the particular deviation, the individual, and the social context.

Substantial possibility of individual role engulfment in a situation in which subcultural elaboration is not very likely is illustrated by the condition of stuttering. Lemert has referred to adult stuttering as representing in many respects the "pure case" of secondary deviance,

> because stuttering thus far has defied efforts at causative explanation. It appears to be exclusively a process-product in which . . . normal speech variations, or at most, minor abnormalities of speech (primary stuttering) can be fed into an interactional or evaluational process and come out as secondary stuttering.[67]

As Lemert has pointed out, early reactions to childhood speech difficulties—on the part of family, peers, schoolteachers, and so on—seem to determine whether or not the difficulty persists and expands. Research findings indicate that merely calling a child a "stutterer" does not necessarily ensure persistent adult stuttering; rather, a substantial elaboration of interaction between the individual's speech difficulties and certain kinds of negative response seems required. Lemert has also observed that the age levels at which various situational pressures are experienced may be an important factor; as a child grows older the primacy of the stuttering role apparently increases. For our purposes, Lemert's comments on the role of speech therapy in fostering, rather than in impeding, the development of secondary stuttering are particularly interesting:

> . . . we may safely say that going to a speech clinic in all cases confronts the individual with a clear-cut societal definition of the stuttering self. The association with other stutterers and with speech cases in the clinic situation has a clear implication for self and role, as well as the knowledge that other students or members of the community know the function of the clinic. One well-known clinic, at a Middle Western college, makes it more or less of a prerequisite for treatment of adult stutterers that they make frank

67 Lemert, *Human Deviance, Social Problems, and Social Control* (Englewood Cliffs, N.J.: Prentice-Hall, 1967), p. 56.

avowals in speech and behavior that they are stutterers. This is done by having the stutterers practice blocks in front of mirrors, exaggerate them, copy one another's blocks, and have or fake blocks in public situations. While there are several objectives behind this procedure, one of its chief consequences is to instill an unequivocal self-definition in the stutterer as one who is different from others. . . .[68]

This passage recalls to our attention the highly significant labeling role played by organizations, to which we now turn once again.

[68] Lemert, *Social Pathology*, p. 159.

four
Labeling and
its consequences in
organizational processing

ORGANIZATIONS produce deviants. Again it should be emphasized that, in making this claim, the labeling analyst is not denying the reality of individual acts of deviation. The study of deviance-processing organizations is, however, vitally necessary for understanding of the ways in which efforts at social control shape and even, in a sense, "cause" deviance outcomes. It should already be quite apparent from our consideration of basic processes in imputation of deviance that organizational responses are among the most pertinent examples of how "others" react to deviation. Particularly by stressing the impact upon the deviator of public identification and response, the labeling approach encourages direct analysis of the organizations that deal with deviating individuals (that try to apprehend them, process them legally, "treat" them, and so on). As we might expect, then, a number of basic themes that have emerged from substantial sociological research on organizations of all kinds are extremely helpful in understanding the processing and "production" of deviance.

For example, the now widely acknowledged sociological claim

that within a formal organizational structure informal patterns of social organization invariably emerge is highly relevant to our purposes. These patterns comprise both structural features (like informal power structure and status hierarchy) and "cultural" features (unofficial norms). The significance of this informal side of organizational life has been brought out by labeling-oriented analyses of various stages in the processing of deviators by control agents and agencies. Egon Bittner's study of the "peace keeping" function of the police on Skid Row has shown how the patrolman's personal knowledge of the area and its residents, informal under- standings that develop between the patrollers and the patrolled, and ad hoc decision-making geared more to the special problems of this sort of police work than to the formal categories of the law shape the official processing of one category of deviators.[1] Simi- larly, David Sudnow's study of a public defender's office[2] has high- lighted the importance of informal working arrangements be- tween appointed defense attorneys and prosecutors in determining the disposition of cases before the criminal courts. Such arrange- ments appear to go beyond the plea bargaining noted earlier to include more general processes of categorizing specific cases (ac- cording to the lawyers' conceptions, or "typifications," of "normal crimes") and gearing desired outcomes to such classifications. As we have already observed about the plea-bargaining studies, con- trol agents' need to maintain a smooth working "system" in such settings is a major determinant of the patterns uncovered in any study of official deviance outcomes (for example, rates of convic- tion, types of sentences received, by offenders in particular social categories). Further documentation of this tendency has been pro- vided in Jerome Skolnick's analysis of the relation between police work and the "criminal court community,"[3] as well as in various

[1] Egon Bittner, "The Police on Skid Row: A Study of Peace Keeping," *American Sociological Review*, 32 (October 1967), 699–715. For further details on relevant processing organizations see Jacqueline Wiseman, *Stations of the Lost: The Treatment of Skid Row Alcoholics* (Englewood Cliffs, N.J.: Prentice-Hall, 1970).

[2] David Sudnow, "Normal Crimes: Sociological Features of the Penal Code in a Public Defender Office," *Social Problems*, 12 (Winter 1965), 255–276.

[3] Jerome Skolnick, *Justice Without Trial* (New York: Wiley, 1966).

studies of the processing of juvenile delinquents to be discussed shortly.

Analyses of residential treatment and correctional institutions have also suggested the significance of informal social organization in shaping deviance-control situations. In his book *Asylums*,[4] Erving Goffman has considered a number of aspects of such informal organization, particularly those that help to maintain the mental hospital as a going concern and at the same time to mediate and soften the impact of this kind of "total institution" in shaping the mental patient's "moral career." Goffman's analysis of the processes by which patients are stripped of identity and mortified is, of course, widely cited as a major examination of status transformation within the context of a residential institution. It should be kept in mind, however, that delineation of the informal organizational patterns at work in the processing of deviators does not always require an explicit labeling orientation. An example of one that is not based on such an orientation may be Gresham Sykes' study of a maximum-security prison, in which, without any special labeling emphasis, the author has clearly depicted (under the rubric "the corruption of authority") the informal bargains struck between jailers and prisoners, bargains that both facilitate the workings of the organization and vitally influence the conditions of the individuals within it.[5]

Nonetheless, it seems that a labeling approach does bring out with special clarity the role of informal organizational forces in shaping the experiences of individuals undergoing formal processing by social-control agencies. Furthermore, as the several studies just cited suggest, labeling analysis permits us to bring together diverse research findings that highlight the role of such forces in different kinds of (or degrees of) organizational structure. We thus see approximately similar development of informal norms as it affects deviance outcomes, both in closed "total institutions," and in somewhat less rigidly structured legal "organizations" con-

[4] Erving Goffman, *Asylums* (Garden City, N.Y.: Doubleday Anchor, 1961).
[5] Gresham Sykes, *The Society of Captives* (Princeton: Princeton University Press, 1958).

cerned with deviation, including even that of police work, although we may not choose to describe rather free-wheeling patrol activities in organizational terms.

Another basic teaching of organizational sociology that emerges clearly in a labeling analysis of deviance and social control involves the ways in which internal and external relations influence an organization's work. The relevance of relations within the organization has already been indicated, though a more systematic breakdown into staff-staff, staff-client, and client-client relations may provide a more nearly complete picture of the significant internal patterns and processes. There are, of course, many kinds of outside forces that may also impinge on the operations of an organization, and many of them are relevant to an analysis of social-control agencies. Some of the most important forces for our purposes are, first, governmental units like legislatures, which may provide the organizational mandate, exert supervision or control, and play an important role in funding and more generally in legitimizing an organization's work; second, other public or private agencies, with which the organization must develop working relations; third, private sources of funding and support; fourth, any relevant "pressure" or "interest" groups; fifth, community or "public" opinion generally and the mass media; sixth, relevant legal provisions, both substantive and procedural; and seventh, relevant "ideologies" like conceptions of "treatment" and "rehabilitation." The significance of many of these external forces can be judged from examples to be presented here.

A third general finding from organizational analysis that has great relevance to the study of deviance is the multiplicity or ambiguity of organizational goals. Organization analysts well know that confusion of goals causes special problems and invariably affects the clients of organizations, especially of agencies and institutions of social control. Undoubtedly the most familiar example is the conflict between custodial and treatment goals in rehabilitation and correctional institutions. This conflict of goals has an internal structural counterpart, of course, in the problems of relations between custodial staff and treatment staff in the same institution; these problems seem to persist under varying degrees of emphasis on custody and treatment.[6]

The tendency for the operations of an organization to become ends in themselves, often called the "displacement of goals," also has considerable importance in analysis of efforts at social control. As we have just seen, the interrelations that develop within a social-control organization tend to take on a momentum of their own. Situations may then arise in which the perceived needs of the organization as such, or of various staff roles within it, become major determinants of the patterns of organizational work (and thus of the ways in which clients are treated).

A final point that should always be kept in mind is that organizations concerned with deviation share with other kinds of organizations all the common practical problems of finances, plant and equipment, recruitment and training of personnel, and the like. In fact, these matters may have special importance because of their influence on the selection of clientele. The disposition of legal cases, the classification of "patients," the particular treatment program to which a specific individual is assigned—such decisions cannot be fully understood in terms of formal legal provisions, technical diagnoses, and determination in depth of "what is best in this particular case" alone. On the contrary, practitioners know only too well that such dispositions often are vitally affected by availability of funds and treatment facilities, as well as by other organizational factors among those that we have been considering.

Organizational imperatives:
two examples

JUVENILE COURTS

The processing of "juvenile delinquents," some aspects of which have already been touched on, nicely illustrates some of the major

[6] See Mayer N. Zald, "The Correctional Institution for Juvenile Offenders: An Analysis of Organizational 'Character,'" *Social Problems*, 8 (Summer 1960), 57–67; see also David Street, Robert Vinter, and Charles Perrow, *Organization for Treatment* (New York: Free Press, 1966).

organizational factors influencing deviance outcomes. Ironically, the juvenile court—largely created by social reformers who sought to curb the early stigmatization of youth in trouble[7]—is a major arena for labeling processes, for the social and to a considerable degree, organizational production of deviants. Over the years critics have noted various features of the juvenile-court system that, though aimed at maximizing informality and flexibility and mini- mizing stigmatization, have actually served to eliminate basic procedural safeguards and to promote inequities. The extremely vague wording of the statutes on "delinquency," the elimination of adversary procedures from the juvenile courts, the very broad discretion of juvenile-court judges, and provisions for indetermi- nate commitment periods (under which the juvenile offender may be sent to a training school or other "treatment institution" for a longer time than if he had committed the same act as an adult) are all examples. As even early critics pointed out—very much in the spirit of the labeling orientation—the euphemistic terminology employed in this system (for example, "adjudication as a delin- quent" instead of "criminal conviction," "training school" instead of "prison") cannot disguise the significant extent to which the "adjudicated delinquent" is in fact stigmatized, punished, and potentially "criminalized." One writer has even argued that the very informality of juvenile-court proceedings themselves, as well as the quite apparent absence of consistency and uniformity in the disposition of specific cases, may promote or reinforce among juvenile offenders a sense of injustice and disrespect for the legal system—which may in turn actually encourage delinquent be- havior.[8]

To a great extent problems arising in the juvenile court are attributable to the substantial discretion vested in control agents at several stages, combined with the multiple or confused goals of the system as a whole. As one commentator has recently stated, "The court is expected simultaneously to preserve the institution

7 See Anthony Platt, *The Child Savers* (Chicago: University of Chicago Press, 1969).
8 David Matza, *Delinquency and Drift* (New York: Wiley, 1966).

of law, to enhance the legitimate interests of its clients, especially those of children, and to serve the welfare of the community while protecting public order." He has also emphasized the juvenile court's involved relations with other organizations at both state and local levels and the fact that it "must maintain complex and multi-level relations in order to achieve stability and effectiveness."[9]

These structural, specifically organizational, problems have been closely analyzed in Robert Emerson's recent study of a juvenile court in a large northern metropolitan area.[10] Both internal staff relations and relations with outside forces and agencies were found to affect the court's work. The procedures, tone, and policies of the court were set by the judges, whose ultimate authority dominated the proceedings. The chief judge had substantial latitude in establishing operating rules and procedures for the court and also served as chief administrator, with power to hire, organize, and oversee court staff, as well as to establish general policies that probation officers were supposed to implement. The balance between informality and procedural safeguards during court hearings depended largely upon the decisions of the chief judge, who had instituted reasonably strict procedures for hearings on the facts of each case and permitted a more informal, social-work approach only after findings of delinquency had been made (in the dispositional phase). A probation officer, appointed by the chief judge, occupied an ambiguous position in this court structure:

> On the one hand, he performs the routine chores which keep the court operation going. His court work provides his occupational identification and elicits a great deal of commitment on his part. On the other hand, the probation officer has low professional status within the court itself, relative to both judges and clinic personnel. Furthermore, he is the organizational subordinate of the judges; probation officers hold their jobs at least partially at the discretion

9 Robert D. Vinter, "The Juvenile Court as an Institution," in President's Commission on Law Enforcement and Administration of Justice, *Task Force Report: Juvenile Delinquency and Youth Crime* (Washington, D.C.: Government Printing Office, 1967), p. 85.

10 Robert M. Emerson, *Judging Delinquents* (Chicago: Aldine, 1969).

of the chief judge, who may dismiss an officer for "cause" subject to review by the Probation Board, and who also directs and evaluates their work. However, the probation officer's practical knowledge and experience tend to offset this low professional and hierarchical standing.[11]

Perhaps it is not surprising, then, that the probation officers minimized the importance of technical and professional competence and considered common sense and intimate knowledge of the local community to be the basic prerequisites for successful probation work. Emerson also examined the roles of defense lawyers (who tended not to favor working in the juvenile court, where adversary procedures were not followed) and of court clinicians (whose psychiatric orientations tended to clash with the conceptions of other court staff, especially the probation officers).

Although the dispositions of the court (the labels that it dispensed) were likely to be shaped by the views of its key personnel and authority structure, they were also subject to substantial influence from external forces. Emerson has noted that the court's close political ties affected its work. All its judges had been appointed by the governor from the local bar and political structure for life terms. None had worked with delinquency or child welfare before appointment to the court. After examining a number of controversies related to the court's work, Emerson has concluded that "politically important segments of the local community, rather than the city's social agencies and social welfare professionals, provide the juvenile court's primary 'constituency.' "[12] For example, the court's general conduct of its work reflected considerable sensitivity to local political forces and community opinion. Furthermore, despite much active lobbying by social-welfare forces for the appointment of a person with professional experience to fill a judicial vacancy, a political ally of the governor was appointed.

The court's relations with the police also vitally influenced its handling of cases. As Emerson has noted, the court had the power to review and to dispose of delinquency complaints initiated by the

11 *Ibid.*, pp. 16–17.
12 *Ibid.*, p. 35.

police. But, at the same time, the court depended upon the police to provide it with cases and also to mediate its relations with the rest of the community. Therefore it had to maintain smooth working relations with the police. Its activities were further affected by the nature of police work with juveniles, which, as Emerson has stressed, involved formal "solving of crimes" less than the handling (largely through informal settlement) of a wide variety of legally ambiguous and relatively minor complaints. Because police work with juveniles consisted to a great extent of such informal mediation and settlement, when the police did bring a case before the juvenile court it was usually one that had been especially troublesome, one in which such informal processes had not "worked." Typically the police demanded stern action in court cases that they initiated, for they believed that in those instances "rehabilitation" (a major goal of the juvenile-court system) had already been tried and had failed. The court staff did depend upon the police to bring cases to its attention, for it believed itself capable of effective preventive action only if it regularly learned of children in trouble. In the court that Emerson studied probation officers and police appeared to have developed good working relations based on mutual dependence and cooperation. This outcome had been facilitated not only by the probation staff's sympathetic appreciation of the problems of the police but also by

> a common lower-middle class Irish background, as well as a tendency for probation officers to be upwardly mobile policemen (two of the court's probation officers came from police backgrounds). It also reflects a common nonprofessional status in a field increasingly preempted by professionals.[13]

These comments suggest some of the extralegal factors that may influence, at least indirectly, the processing of youths through the juvenile-court system. Perhaps particularly interesting is Emerson's emphasis on the court's major role as what he has called a "back up institution." It was expected to handle problems that other community institutions had not been able to handle, and consequently it was under continual pressure to apply and enforce

[13] *Ibid.,* p. 47.

negative labels that had already been invoked by other agencies (a pressure that ran counter to the juvenile-court ideology of avoiding stigmatization of youth whenever possible). As Emerson has pointed out, critics of the court's stigmatizing role should keep in mind this context of pressures:

> In part the juvenile court produces delinquents by validating the prior judgments and demands for action of local institutions encountering problems of control from troublesome youths. The juvenile court's label represents the end product of the efforts of such institutions to deal with troublesome cases. From this perspective, the juvenile court not only labels delinquents, but it also *resists labeling* by refusing to validate complainants' judgments and to follow their proposed course of action. This suggests that the goal of minimizing court stigmatization requires not only limiting court jurisdiction and power by holding it to a doctrine of "judicious non-intervention" [suggested by Edwin Lemert in a recent critique of the juvenile court], but also maximizing its power and inclination to resist and change established definitions and proscriptions about delinquents and their situations.[14]

AGENCIES FOR THE BLIND

A second major illustration of the impact of organizational imperatives is the operation of what Robert Scott has called "the blindness system." We have already considered some aspects of social reactions to the blind; the "creation" of blind men by blindness organizations represents an elaboration and exacerbation of such reactions. After noting that the general definition of blindness is somewhat arbitrary and that in fact the majority of people classified as blind have at least some measurable vision, Scott has analyzed a complex, organized socialization system through which many people who can actually see a little come to feel and act as if they cannot. He notes that such socialization occurs in two stages: recruitment and participation in the agency programs themselves.[15]

[14] *Ibid.*, p. 275.
[15] Robert A. Scott, *The Making of Blind Men* (New York: Russell Sage, 1969), chaps. 3–5.

Scott has observed, first, that such organizations cater over-whelmingly to blind children and to adults before old age; few services are available for the large category of the aged blind or for the multiple-handicapped. The necessity of careful eye examinations for determining legal blindness also has important implications for recruiting. Some people who would be adjudged blind after such examinations never take them and thus never gain access to services for the blind. Others define themselves as blind because of difficulties that they encounter, and then voluntarily seek help either from medical specialists or from blindness agencies. But, as Scott has stressed, those who are labeled blind by others can rarely simply decide what they want to do about their conditions. On the contrary, they are under great pressure from welfare and medical specialists, as well as from family and friends, to think of themselves as "blind." Once an ophthalmologist has determined that an individual is blind, according to Scott, he often takes the position that nothing further can be done medically and refers the individual to a welfare agency. This approach

> is subjectively experienced by the person who is legally blind as an abrupt redefinition of his problem. Whereas he was previously treated as a sighted person who had difficulty seeing, he is now treated as a blind person who has residual vision.[16]

This redefinition is strengthened by his experiences in a blindness agency:

> Such persons may be expected to learn braille, even though special lenses would enable them to read ordinary or enlarged ink print. Often they are given the same training in the use of mechanical aids for mobility as totally blind persons, even though the remaining vision would enable them to continue doing the jobs they have always done.[17]

Scott has noted further that the person undergoing socialization into this blindness role is often confronted with consensus on this

16 *Ibid.*, p. 73.
17 *Ibid.*, p. 74.

redefinition among those around him, a consensus that is reinforced by an exaggerated public confidence in the competence of blindness agencies to help all blind people.

Of the agency programs themselves, Scott has declared that personnel tend to hold notions about blindness different from those of newly blind people. They view blindness as "one of the most severe of all handicaps, the effects of which are long-lasting, pervasive, and extremely difficult to ameliorate," and they insist, subtly or not so subtly, that their clients adopt the same view. How the blind person himself feels about his disability and what he thinks that he can accomplish despite it are often ignored, or at least resisted, by such workers. The client is under great pressure to accept the agency's definition of his problem and may not be permitted to continue in more advanced stages of the agency program unless he shows such "insight."

Scott has distinguished between two major approaches that may be adopted by blindness organizations: the restorative approach, resting on the premise that many blind people can be restored to high levels of independence and can thus be expected to lead fairly normal lives, and the accommodative approach, the premise of which is that such independence is an unrealistic goal for most blind people. Scott has found that, though almost all agencies express approval of the restorative ideal, most adopt an accommodative approach in practice. When the emphasis is accommodative, even the physical arrangements may reflect such an orientation:

> In some agencies, for example, the elevators have tape recorders that report the floor at which the elevator is stopping and the direction in which it is going, and panels of braille numbers for each floor as well. Other agencies have mounted over their front doors special bells that ring at regular intervals to indicate to blind people that they are approaching the building. Many agencies maintain fleets of cars to pick up clients at their homes and bring them to the agency for services. In the cafeterias of many agencies, special precautions are taken to serve only food that blind people can eat without awkwardness. In one agency

cafeteria, for example, the food is cut before it is served, and only spoons are provided.[18]

Although such devices are intriguing and probably very well intended, their potential contribution to developing in the blind person an incapacity for independence should be obvious (an interesting illustration of the role that physical setting and objects may play in labeling). Indeed, as Scott has suggested, these agencies seem to assume that eventually most clients will completely organize their lives around agency routine; as the person who is fully socialized in such a system will almost inevitably be unable to adjust to life in the outside community, there seems to be no really tenable alternative.

Although staff beliefs and organizational ideologies contribute significantly to pressures for accommodation, Scott has also noted that certain outside pressures are partly responsible for this tendency. Blindness agencies tend, for example, to be very well funded, and one reason is public approval of (or covert demand for) accommodative programs. Such programs mesh well with the strong avoidance tendencies exhibited by the sighted toward the blind. These tendencies are so strong, Scott has suggested, that any agency that were to concentrate on the ideal of reintegrating the blind into general community life might well have difficulty securing adequate funds. We can thus see a circular process at work: Community attitudes lead to accommodative agency orientations, which in turn have distinct effects upon the behavior and self-concepts of the clients, which in turn uphold and reinforce the pre-existing attitudes of the sighted.

Other relevant organizational factors cited by Scott include competition for clients (which leads agencies to stress the accommodative approach, through which it is likely to secure a stable, long-term clientele) and the vested interests of certain workers in existing agency programs. There is a group of workers who have little or no formal training and whose claims to expertise rest solely on many years of practical experience working with the

18 *Ibid.,* pp. 84–85.

blind. Scott has observed that, though many of these workers are highly competent and sensitive specialists, they do not have the professional security and mobility of the formally trained and academically certified workers. As a consequence, "Their power and influence are tied to the specific organizations whose ranks they control, and their status therefore depends heavily upon the continued functioning of the agency with which they are identified."[19] Such vested interests, then, clearly inhibit agency flexibility and innovation.

We have already remarked that not all blind people need accept the "approved" blindness role, though usually some special resources are necessary to resist it. From an organizational point of view, a particularly interesting category is that of blinded veterans. Very substantial provision has been made for such people, both financially and through the development of comprehensive rehabilitation programs (largely restorative in nature). It is therefore interesting that what systematic comparisons have been attempted have revealed that blind veterans manage much better than do other blind people. They tend to have higher incomes, to be more active in organizations not related to blindness, to have more friends who are not blind, to be less isolated, and so on. As Scott has commented, "These data indicate in a very striking way how alternative approaches to rehabilitation can produce radically different socialization outcomes among blind people."[20]

Organizational impact

Analysis of the public and other organizations that deal with deviating individuals makes clear that "what may be and usually is a crisis and an emergency to the person experiencing this official processing is, from the point of view of the official and the agency for which he works, simply a matter of organizational routine." This fact partly determines

19 *Ibid.*, p. 102.
20 *Ibid.*, p. 116.

the nature of the processing itself and thus indirectly what happens to the individuals who are processed. From one point of view, then, as Earl Rubington and Martin Weinberg have gone on to emphasize, problems of management are central to deviance control. What is really happening at the organizational level of analysis is the bureaucratization of deviance; "deviants come under the regulation of hierarchy, impersonality, specialization, and systematic formal rules."[21]

Organizational efforts to "manage" deviance affect deviation situations in many significant ways. One is the initial selection from the general population of these specific individuals who are going to be "processed" (the implementing of what Kai Erikson has called the "community screen"). Stereotyping, or typification, is a significant element in this screening process. An excellent example can be found in Irving Piliavin and Scott Briar's study of police encounters with juveniles, in which they stress the officer's great discretion to choose among various actions and dispositions:

> . . . both the decision made in field—whether or not to bring the boy in—and the decision made at the station—which disposition to invoke—were based largely on cues which emerged from the interaction between the officer and the youth, cues from which the officer inferred the youth's character. These cues included the youth's group affiliations, age, race, grooming, dress, and demeanor. Older juveniles, members of known delinquent gangs, Negroes, youths with well-oiled hair, black jackets, and soiled denims or jeans (the presumed uniform of "tough" boys), and boys who in their interactions with officers did not manifest what were considered to be appropriate signs of respect tended to receive the more severe dispositions.[22]

As other examples have already shown us, some kind of "typing," of classification into "normal cases," almost invariably develops from control agents' need to operate the organization at an efficient level. Obviously this need seriously affects the fates of

21 Earl Rubington and Martin S. Weinberg, eds., *Deviance: The Interactionist Perspective* (New York: Macmillan, 1968), p. 111.
22 Irving Piliavin and Scott Briar, "Police Encounters with Juveniles," *American Journal of Sociology*, 69 (September 1964), 210.

suspects or identified deviators. Individuals in certain social categories or those exhibiting more or fewer characteristics of the predetermined "types" face varying probabilities (varying "categoric risks," in an actuarial sense) of being dealt with in one or another of the prescribed ways.

Another major consequence of organizational imperatives is that they significantly influence the substantive and procedural development of organizational programs. This observation applies to what may be called "internal" programs (as in blindness organizations and in "total institutions" for the treatment of the mentally ill or the "correction" of criminal offenders) and to the somewhat less "institutional" processing mechanisms of the criminal-court system and related legal bodies.

One aspect of this development involves the shaping of systematic machinery by which individuals are passed along from one stage to the next (Rubington and Weinberg have called it a "deviance corridor"). This point is illustrated by the set of social-control processes and organizations relating to troublesome juveniles, who may be identified first in the schools, then screened and perhaps charged by the police, then processed by the juvenile courts, then committed to juvenile-treatment institutions. Clearly, a selection process of sorts occurs at each stage, for not all those at any one stage are passed on to the next; it is important to study the factors associated with such selections. Perhaps equally important is that there is likely to be a complex or sequence of organizations involved in processing particular kinds of deviation. And, although it is true that the factors determining outcomes at one stage in the sequence may differ from those most clearly operating at another stage, there is likely to be a tendency toward consistency among selection criteria as an overall processing "system" develops. We may thus properly speak of a "delinquency-processing system," a "blindness system," and the like.

Yet another result of the organizational processes, one that is, however, implicit in the results already considered, is reflected in official data on deviance. Social-control agencies produce statistics. John Kitsuse and Aaron Cicourel have suggested that we should not dismiss completely the official statistics on deviance, even though they are obviously faulty and incomplete indications of the actual extent and distribution of deviating acts. From a labeling point of view, however, we may be most interested in the role of social-control agencies in a "rate-producing process."[23] The definitions and criteria applied by the processing organizations may not be those that the sociologist would accept as "valid" or "fair"; nonetheless they constitute a quite real and very important factor in the production of deviance outcomes. Rates of deviance do not simply exist in the abstract. They are produced through the work of organizations. In one sense, public statistics on deviance reflect initial public reactions to particular kinds of deviation implemented and mediated through various control processes and organizations. At the same time a kind of feedback mechanism is probably also at work. Statistics that do become known to the general public very likely influence common conceptions of the nature of particular deviance problems, and these conceptions in turn help to determine how the public reacts to the deviations in question. We should also remember that control organizations sometimes attempt to influence public conceptions of and policies toward problems of deviation directly. Then the vested interests of the organizations and the contents of organizational ideologies may have direct impacts on public reactions.

A final aspect of the organizational processing of deviance, one that we have already discussed at some length, is the direct impact on processed individuals of organizational setting and programs. Such impact is perhaps most clearly apparent in the total institution, as in the typical processes of identity stripping and role engulfment that we have mentioned. John Lofland has mentioned "role-distance denial" in connection with "formal deviant places" (mental hospitals, prisons, and the like). In contrast to "normal" life, which "abounds in small expressions by persons of their incomplete acceptance of arrangements in which they are enmeshed," life in the total institution affords little if any room

---

[23] See John I. Kitsuse and Aaron V. Cicourel, "A Note on the Use of Official Statistics," *Social Problems,* 11 (Fall 1963), 131–139.

for such face-saving and morale-preserving detachment from imposed identities.[24] Again the nature and extent of a particular individual's resources partly determine the degree to which he can fend off this enveloping process.

As we have seen, organizational ideologies, specific details of treatment programs, the very fact of being in a "total" institution, aspects of the physical setting itself, and indirectly the strictly organizational imperatives may all contribute in some way to the imputation of deviant character and the undermining of favorable self-concepts among the organization's clients. Yet, as our examination of the blindness system should have made clear, these effects are not limited to closed residential institutions. Furthermore, Goffman's concept of "moral career" suggests that the impact of organizational processing upon the individual "deviant" usually occurs not all at once but over a period of time and in a succession of stages. In well-developed deviant self-concepts, a number of different organizational settings and programs may have taken their toll singly and in combination. One merit of a labeling-oriented analysis is that, in focusing directly on the ways in which the individual is affected, it makes possible a sensitive appreciation of these complex impacts. Such complexity is suggested by Jacqueline Wiseman's comment on the Skid Row drinker's perception of the system of alcoholic rehabilitation agencies and programs, through which he is likely to have passed.

> He sees a far more complicated and contradictory structure than does the most sophisticated screening and referral agent or professional staff person limited to the confines of his "station" on the loop. The down-and-out drunk has mobility (some of it enforced), and he can experience many correctional and therapeutic approaches. Officials at each station, as in the fable of the seven blind men and the elephant, usually experience only *their* portion of the total constellation. It would take a discussion with the elephant to explain to these persons how it feels to be worked on by seven blind men in succession.[25]

24 John Lofland, *Deviance and Identity* (Englewood Cliffs, N.J.: Prentice-Hall, 1969), p. 170.
25 Wiseman, *op. cit.*, p. 61.

five
Labeling and
its consequences in
collective rule-making

As we pointed out in Chapter Two, critics of the labeling approach have argued that, though labeling analysts stress the importance of societal reactions, they do not really explain them. Yet this criticism is at least partly mistaken. More than most other orientations toward studying deviance, the labeling approach does pose a host of significant questions for research on the rule-making process. Even though we do not yet have a large body of findings (for the "interactionists" admittedly have concentrated their attention upon the effects of labeling, rather than upon the creation of labels), deviance analysis is increasingly turning in this direction. Furthermore, some sociologists, to whom contemporary analysts of deviance might well look for guidelines, long ago emphasized the vital significance of rule-making (as in the early statements by Willard Waller and Edwin Sutherland). At any rate, the relative paucity of data on collective rule-making processes is attributable less to the shortcomings of the approach represented by Becker and his colleagues than to the relative inattention to such processes by sociologists in general, perhaps largely because of early preoccupation with direct study of rule-breaking individuals.

In trying to understand collective rule-making, we may find it useful to take as a point of departure Becker's insistence that enforcement is not automatic or inevitable when behavior violates a rule. As he has properly emphasized, there is no self-regulating social mechanism that provides for such an inevitable reaction: ". . . we cannot say that 'society' is harmed by every infraction and acts to restore the balance."[1] On the contrary, he has argued, rules tend to be enforced only when something provokes enforcement: Someone must take the initiative. Enforcement is an enterprising act, requiring "moral entrepreneurs." Perhaps we can broaden this notion a bit, going beyond, or behind, specific enforcement to the more basic issue of what the operative rules *are*. As no single set of rules or norms referring either to specific kinds of behavior or to behavior generally is accepted by everyone in a complex modern society, the degree of initiative or enterprise exerted on behalf of particular rules (declaring their importance, enforcing them, and so on) in a sense helps to determine which rules are dominant or operative in the first place. We can thus picture enterprise or initiative as determining enforcement and enforcement in turn as determining the "real" rules. This ordering is one that we do not usually consider; we typically picture rules as preceding, if not determining, enforcement patterns. Of course rules are central to other issues as well. For example, even rules that are more or less unenforced may still serve important symbolic functions, though presumably there would still have to be at least some initiative in asserting the value of the rules.

Rules, values, and moral crusades

A pivotal question involves the relative importance of social values and personal or group interests in generating rules and rule-enforcement. Although there is some dispute over whether or not there is a coherent system of "dominant values" in any society (more specifically in American

---

1 Howard S. Becker, *Outsiders* (New York: Free Press, 1964), p. 122.

society), at the very least we know that even values generally held to be important in guiding action often conflict with one another in specific situations and as regards "choices" or "policy decisions" that determine what we may call the "prevailing normative order." As Becker has pointed out, general values are poor guides to action:

> People shape values into specific rules in problematic situations. They perceive some area of their existence as troublesome or difficult, requiring action. After considering [perhaps unconsciously, we may add] the various values to which they subscribe, they select one or more of them as relevant to their difficulties and deduce from it a specific rule. The rule, framed to be consistent with the value, states with relative precision which actions are approved and which forbidden, the situations to which the rule is applicable, and the sanctions attached to breaking it.[2]

Of course, some rules (like legal rules) are more explicit than are others (like generally accepted ground rules, informal norms, and so on). The important point, however, is that values do not automatically generate specific rules.

For example, there is wide subscription to the notion that "freedom" is a basic value of modern American life. Yet we can all think of many situations calling for rules in which it is not at all certain just which kinds of freedom should be permitted and which disallowed. A basic reason for this confusion, of course, is that ordinarily enhancement of "freedom" for some implies restriction on the "freedom" of others. Another is that freedom is not the only value shaping such decisions; that is, the meaning of the value of freedom in specific situations depends upon its relations to other values. What forms of political dissent (or deviation) should be permitted in the name of freedom of speech? When, if ever, does political protest begin to infringe on the freedom of others in ways that create a conflict of freedoms? Should an individual be allowed the freedom to harm himself or even to kill himself? The key point of these and many similar examples is simply that the value "freedom" does not automatically produce

2 *Ibid.*, p. 131.

specific rules. On the contrary, it may be that only through the rules that do emerge and gain support can we assess the meaning of freedom as a value in a particular society. Indeed, as Becker has stressed, not only are general values uncertain producers of specific rules, but often the rule-making process may also have retroactive effects on the invoking of values. As he has pointed out:

> a rule may be drawn up simply to serve someone's special interest and a rationale for it later found in some general value. In the same way, a spontaneous act of enforcement may be legitimized by creating a rule to which it can be related. In these cases, the formal relation of general to specific is preserved, even though the time sequence has been altered.[3]

Joseph Gusfield, in his studies of the temperance movement, has focused on another aspect of rule-making, the symbolic component. The moral crusade of the temperance advocates involved a significant dimension of social status. In the subculture of nineteenth-century rural American Protestants, adherence to temperance ideals became a status symbol, and the success or failure of such ideals came to be viewed as symbolic of the success or failure of an entire group and its way of life. As Gusfield has commented, to focus on social-status aspects is not to deny that moral and religious principles may also underlie such crusades. But "religious motives and moral fervor do not happen *in vacuo,* apart from a specific setting." In this particular instance the important social conditions were related to

> . . . the development of threats to the socially dominant position of the Temperance adherent by those whose style of life differs from his. As his own claim to social respect and honor are diminished, the sober, abstaining citizen seeks for public acts through which he may reaffirm the dominance and prestige of his style of life. Converting the sinner to virtue is one way; law is another. Even if the law is not enforced or enforceable, the symbolic import of its passage is important to the reformer. It settles the controversies between those who represent clashing cultures. The

[3] *Ibid.,* p. 134.

public support of one conception of morality at the expense of another enhances the prestige and self-esteem of the victors and degrades the culture of the losers.[4]

According to Gusfield, rule-making generally has a symbolic component. In particular, a rule that has been enacted into law asserts particular norms and values and confers prestige and respect on their adherents. The nature of efforts at moral reform similarly depends upon the extent to which the reformist group's norms and values receive general support. Gusfield has distinguished between assimilative reform (which seeks to improve individuals) and coercive reform (which seeks to force individuals to act in the desired way). When the reformer's own social status and way of life are secure, he will view the norm violator as a "deviant" deserving help. When they are threatened he is more likely to view the violator as an "enemy," a challenger of the legitimacy of the norm who cannot be converted or reformed but must instead be forcibly subdued. Gusfield has depicted a shift in the temperance movement from a predominantly assimilative emphasis to an increasingly coercive one. As long as the social position of those upholding temperance norms was dominant, they could afford to adopt a "humanitarian" approach. But as a conflict of subcultures heightened (a rural, Protestant, middle-class subculture versus an urban, Roman Catholic and secularist, working-class subculture) and the social dominance of the rural Protestants became uncertain, the movement became increasingly embroiled in general normative conflict; the result was a resort to coercive reform measures (Prohibition). Such measures could at least provide symbolic support for the status of the threatened groups.[5]

This emphasis upon the symbolic aspects of rules should not, however, divert our attention from important organizational factors in rule-making. Becker has discussed the ways in which a moral crusade may become institutionalized:

What started as a drive to convince the world of the moral necessity of a new rule finally becomes an organization devoted to the

[4] Joseph Gusfield, *Symbolic Crusade* (Urbana: University of Illinois Press, 1963), pp. 4–5.
[5] *Ibid.*, chaps. 2–4.

enforcement of the rule. Just as radical political movements turn into organized political parties and lusty evangelical sects become staid religious denominations, the final outcome of the moral crusade is a police force.[6]

He has remarked further that interest in maintaining the organization and in keeping a job may become more important to the rule-enforcer than is the moral issue itself.

Donald Dickson has recently suggested that, whereas individual initiative and enterprise often spur moral crusades, at times the moral crusader may be the product of a morally committed bureaucracy rather than its creator. Rule-enforcing organizations, perhaps particularly governmental ones (Dickson's study focused on the Federal Narcotics Bureau), must justify their work and their very existence, and this necessity may in large measure shape their activities.[7] Sometimes, then, the individual moral entrepreneur may act on the basis of organizational interests rather than personal moral outrage and reformist zeal. This interpretation is, of course, quite consistent with our earlier comments on organizational factors in deviant-processing agencies.

At any rate, it is worth stressing that collective rule-making, whether it is derived from the efforts of individual moral entrepreneurs, organizational needs, or other sources, does not simply arise automatically "out of the blue." On the contrary, rules arise from (and can be fully understood only in) terms of the complex sociocultural setting. At least three aspects of this setting usually warrant examination: the general social forces that permit (or "create") categorization of a particular kind of behavior as "deviant," the sequence of events culminating in specific efforts at rule-making and rule-enforcement, and the rule-making processes themselves, for example, legislative debates, hearings, and commission reports. It is important to note, in connection with the first aspect, that there must be public consciousness of a particular "category" of behavior (conscious classification, singling out of specific acts as troublesome and requiring special attention) if rules are to be made

---

[6] Becker, *op. cit.*, pp. 155–156.
[7] Donald T. Dickson, "Bureaucracy and Morality: An Organizational Perspective on a Moral Crusade," *Social Problems,* 16 (Fall 1968), 143–156.

in response. Such categories must, then, be in a sense "created"; they have not always existed "all along." Indeed, in the strictest sense there was no such thing as "juvenile delinquency" before the development of the juvenile court, and "mental illness" as a technical classification is partly a "product" of the mental-health movement.[8]

Another example of the "creation" of deviance categories is that of the "sexual psychopath," which also illustrates our second aspect: that the rule-making process usually involves a sequence of events, rather than occurring in one fell swoop. In his analysis of the passage of legislation against sexual psychopaths Sutherland has described three major stages: arousal of fear in the community by a few serious sex crimes in quick succession, "agitated activity of the community" related to this fear, and the appointment of a committee to marshall the "facts" and to make recommendations. From his examination of the experience in many states, Sutherland has concluded that, "although the general fear subsides within a few days, a committee has the formal duty of following through until positive action is taken. Terror which does not result in a committee is much less likely to result in a law."[9] Sutherland has also pointed out the way in which stereotyping operates at the level of collective rule-making:

> Implicit in these laws is a series of propositions which have been made explicit in an extensive popular literature, namely, that the present danger to women and children from serious sex crimes is very great, for the number of sex crimes is large and is increasing more rapidly than any other crime; that most sex crimes are committed by "sexual degenerates," "sex fiends," or "sexual psychopaths," and that these persons persist in their sexual crimes throughout life; that they always give warning that they are dangerous by first committing minor offenses; that any psychiatrist can diagnose them with a high degree of precision at an early age, before they have committed serious sex crimes; and that

8 See Anthony Platt, *The Child Savers* (Chicago: University of Chicago Press, 1969); see also Thomas S. Szasz, *The Manufacture of Madness* (New York: Harper & Row, 1970).
9 Edwin H. Sutherland, "The Diffusion of Sexual Psychopath Laws," *American Journal of Sociology*, 56 (September 1950), 145.

sexual psychopaths who are diagnosed and identified should be
confined as irresponsible persons until they are pronounced by
psychiatrists to be completely and permanently cured of their
malady.[10]

As Sutherland has pointed out, most of these propositions are
either demonstrably false or highly questionable. Nevertheless
their impact on public policy has been considerable.

In a specific area of norm violation, then, events occurring at
several stages of a sequence tend to feed into one another and
must be considered as representing important contingencies affecting rule-making outcomes. The same is true of the specific
procedures involved in formal rule-making itself. Pamela Roby, in
a detailed analysis of the processes by which a change in the New
York State law on prostitution was effected (she found five distinct
"stages" in the formulation and enforcement of this particular
statutory revision), has noted that a small number of highly interested organizations and individuals used legislative hearings
and commission deliberations to exert substantial influence on the
eventual outcome.[11] The shortsighted tendency of sociologists has
been to leave both chronological and largely descriptive detailing
of such processes, as well as analysis in terms of "pressure groups,"
to their colleagues in political science. By recalling to sociological
attention the political nature of deviance situations (particularly
at the level of collective rule-making), the labeling approach
should promote more comprehensive and realistic analysis in this
area.

Deviance and conflict

A focus on social reactions to
deviance also highlights the close relation that frequently exists
between deviation, on one hand, and patterns of social conflict and

---

[10] *Ibid.*, p. 142.

[11] Pamela A. Roby, "Politics and Criminal Law: Revision of the New York
State Penal Law on Prostitution," *Social Problems*, 17 (Summer 1969),
83–109.

Table 2   *Conflict situations: dimensions of the character and relations of parties in conflict*

RESULTING POPULAR DEFINITION OF THE CONFLICT SITUATION	SIZE AND ORGANIZATION OF PARTY FEARED	ECONOMIC AND POLITICAL POWER OF PARTY FEARED RELATIVE TO PARTY FEARING	DEGREE TO WHICH THE WELL-OR-GANIZED OPPOSING LARGE MINORITY OR MAJORITY FEELS FEAR-FUL OR THREATENED
Deviance ("crime," etc.)	*Individual or small, loosely organized groups*	*Almost none*	*Very high*
Civil uprising or disorder	*Small, loosely organized groups*	*Relatively low*	*Very high*
Social movement	*Sizeable organized minority*	*Relatively low*	*Mild*
Civil war	*Large, well-organized minority*	*Relatively high or almost equal*	*Very high*
Mainstream party politics in the United States	*Large, organized minority*	*About equal*	*Mild*

SOURCE: John Lofland, *Deviance and Identity* (Englewood Cliffs, N.J.: Prentice-Hall, 1969), p. 15.

change on the other. Table 2 illustrates John Lofland's argument that whether or not a situation is considered as deviant, rather than simply as a social movement or a political conflict, depends upon various configurations of power, fear, and threat. The crucial point, according to Lofland, is "the dynamics of what proportion of a society, how well organized and how powerful, are fearful of, and feel threatened by, some other portion of the society." Similarly, he has observed that "the imputation of even greatly feared acts and persons as deviant seems to depend less upon particular behavior per se than upon the respective size, degree of power, and degree of organization of parties to an issue."[12]

Of course, to focus on the power factor is not to deny the significance of either the values held by conflicting groups or the substance of the behavior involved. In a sense, we want to explain *under what circumstances* a powerful element in society becomes fearful of or feels threatened by other elements. The answer to that question cannot be framed solely in terms of relative amounts of power, fear, and threat. Lofland has also highlighted ambiguity as a central factor in fearfulness and the sense of threat. As he has commented, physical harm, financial loss, and so on do not by any means exhaust the possible sources of these feelings. People wish also to be protected against disruptive ambiguity and unreasonable contingencies. This wish may be one reason for considering the physically handicapped and the blind as deviant; the anxiety and ambiguity created by their conditions are threatening to "normals" and produce reactions defining deviance.

Without doubt Lofland is correct in his statement that for a given type of behavior to be effectively defined as deviant at least a sizable minority must feel threatened by it; almost any act or person seems threatening to *some* element in a society. Yet, even allowing the cogency of Lofland's analysis, such criteria as size and organization (of both threatening and threatened elements) hardly provide secure bases for clear-cut distinctions between deviance and its absence. Again it seems that the kind of contingent or conditional definition that we offered earlier (in which behavior is defined as deviant *to the extent that* certain reactions occur) offers some real advantages. Admittedly, if those who fear or feel threatened by specific behavior have no hope at all of controlling the definition of the situation, then it may be meaningless to consider calling the threatening behavior "deviant." But they rarely are so powerless; usually the power of the conflicting elements to assert their definitions varies in degree, not absolutely.

Indeed, it is most significant sociologically—and even to some

[12] John Lofland, *Deviance and Identity* (Englewood Cliffs, N.J.: Prentice-Hall, 1969), pp. 13, 15.

extent recognized in everyday life—that various forms of behavior are simultaneously viewed by some members of a society as "deviant" and by others as "political" or "social" movements. That such definitions can coexist, each with a certain amount of social force, is a major reason why it is impossible to settle on a neat, mutually exclusive classification. A most useful point to keep in mind, actually, is that, whenever the legitimacy of specific norms is explicitly challenged, we find a struggle between those who seek to define the issue as political (as a clash between social movements) and those who seek to define it as one of individual deviance (as wrongdoing, sickness, and the like). Such struggles do not have clear-cut starting and stopping points, and they do not produce unalterable outcomes. It is in the very nature of the struggle that the relative strengths of competing definitions are constantly shifting.

The mixed reactions to, and definitions of, contemporary "youth culture" nicely illustrate this point. On one hand, there are those who view a combination of the political and social activities of young people today—including political radicalism, drug use, rock music, and so on—as indications of a genuine social movement, a search for an "alternative life style," a significant "counter-culture."[13] On the other hand, there are those who consider such characterizations and blanket references to "the movement" as an unwarranted lumping together and "politicizing" of what they believe to be basically unrelated patterns of individual "deviance." As long as these definitions are in continuous conflict, it is clearly impossible to state definitively which of the two kinds of phenomena the behavior in question "actually is." The social meaning of the various activities is in dispute, and their social standing is continually undergoing change. Under such circumstances we simply cannot treat as completely separable entities the aspects of the situation that might be labeled "deviance," "conflict," and "change."

In his already classic discussion of reference-group theory, Robert Merton has drawn a useful distinction between ordinary

[13] See Theodore Roszak, *The Making of a Counter Culture* (Garden City, N.Y.: Doubleday, 1969).

deviance and nonconformity. Merton hoped to set apart, under the latter term, those failures or refusals to conform in which there is fairly explicit reference to alternative norms. He appears to have had in mind mainly political nonconformity, as contrasted with criminal activity, especially professional crime. Merton claimed that, in contrast to the criminal, the nonconformist proclaims his deviations, challenges the legitimacy of the norms or at least their applicability to certain situations, aims to change the prevailing norms, and typically appeals to higher morality. Most significantly, according to Merton, the nonconformist elicits a special response from others:

> . . . the nonconformist is, however reluctantly and subconsciously, assumed to depart from prevailing norms for wholly or largely disinterested purposes; the criminal is assumed to deviate from the norms in order to serve his own interests.[14]

Merton also argued that different motivations are probably at work in the two instances and in particular that blanket application of psychological explanations would be misleading. This point may be important for our purposes, for there is a substantial tendency in modern American society to apply psychological interpretations to all kinds of deviating behavior, including political deviation, or what Merton called "nonconformity." As the acceptance of behavior as nonconforming does seem to give it special standing and as the alternative definition of behavior as deviant tends to stigmatize individuals, psychological "explanations" in some borderline behavior areas may well represent efforts to denigrate (to "put down," in the current idiom) what might otherwise be considered respectable political or social movements and activities. Merton did point out the danger of viewing all nonconformity as socially dysfunctional: ". . . it is not infrequently the case that the nonconforming minority in a society represents the interests and ultimate values of the group more effectively than the conforming majority."[15]

14 Robert K. Merton, *Social Theory and Social Structure* (rev. ed.; New York: Free Press, 1959), p. 361.
15 *Ibid.*, p. 367.

As some of the comments in this section may already have suggested, it is becoming increasingly difficult to maintain a sharp distinction between deviant behavior and social conflict. This point has been emphasized recently by Irving Horowitz and Martin Liebowitz, who have claimed that, whereas our society has been inclined to view deviation from the point of view of a "consensus" model (and to evaluate it in therapeutic, rather than political, terms), real elements of conflict often underlie it. "As the politicization of deviance develops, the hidden conflict will become visible and deviants can be expected to demand changes in the configuration of the social hierarchy."[16] They have argued that the distinction between political marginality and social deviance is now obsolete and have noted, on one hand, a growing tendency for such deviators as homosexuals and drug addicts to organize to further their "interests" and, on the other, the increasing incorporation into political activity of acts of individual "deviance."

A major contribution to our understanding of these complex relations is a recent essay by Ralph Turner, "The Public Perception of Protest."[17] Turner has developed a kind of "labeling" analysis of recent racial disturbances, emphasizing that public reactions to a disturbance crucially affect its course and recurrence, as well as the specific control policies that it evokes. To be publicly credible as social protest, rather than being disapproved as a disturbance, it must display characteristics consistent with preconceptions of what legitimate protest is "like":

> To be credible as protestors, troublemakers must seem to constitute a major part of a group whose grievances are already well documented, who are believed to be individually or collectively powerless to correct their grievances, and who show some signs of moral virtue that render them "deserving." Any indication that only few participated or felt sympathy with the disturbances pre-

16 Irving Louis Horowitz and Martin Liebowitz, "Social Deviance and Political Marginality: Toward a Redefinition of the Relation Between Sociology and Politics," *Social Problems,* 15 (Winter 1968), 282.
17 Ralph H. Turner, "The Public Perception of Protest," *American Sociological Review,* 34 (December 1969), 815–831.

disposes observers to see the activities as deviance or as revolutionary activity by a small cadre of agitators.[18]

Similarly, the group must have been ordinarily law-abiding, and the protest must seem spontaneous (or, if organized, as having "gotten out of hand") and as unmotivated by desire for personal gain. As Turner has further noted, the interpretation of a disturbance as protest implies an admission of injustice, an admission that can be made with greater ease by some segments of society than by others.

> . . . groups that are clearly advantaged by comparison with the "protestors" can find the claim of injustice more credible than groups less advantaged. . . . Consequently, the great middle segment of American population finds it easier to identify black ghetto disturbances as social protest than to interpret college student demonstrations in the same sense. Similarly, black student demonstrations are less amenable to interpretation as protest than ghetto demonstrations.
>
> According to this view, groups who see themselves as even more disadvantaged than the protestors are least likely to grant their claim. Viewed from below, disturbances are most easily comprehended as power plays or as deviance.[19]

Turner has also analyzed numerous other subtle features of such situations, but for our purposes the main point is simply that once again in racial disturbances we see the vital significance of the meanings that people attach to behavior. The actions in question are not automatically and unquestionably classifiable as "protest," "deviance," or "rebellion." The meanings that people construct around events determine "what" the outcome "is."

Conclusion

In the last three chapters we have sought neither to provide an encyclopedic review of all recent

18 *Ibid.*, p. 818.
19 *Ibid.*, pp. 819–820.

studies undertaken from a labeling perspective nor to consider every aspect and consequence of labeling processes. Instead we have sought merely to spell out and illustrate the major processes and levels of analysis highlighted by a labeling approach. We have seen that such an approach replaces earlier individually oriented preoccupations with new attention to processes of definition and their consequences. This approach involves a shift in emphasis from the deviation itself to the social-control efforts directed toward it. We have stressed the broad scope and applicability of labeling analysis. Although special attention has been paid to social-psychological consequences for the individual of being defined and treated as a "deviant," we have also seen that both general deviance situations and individual deviant careers can properly be viewed as "outcomes" of labeling processes. The term "secondary deviance" can thus be broadly interpreted to include the secondary, situational effects of labeling particular behavior negatively. The entire area of borderline crime abounds in illustrations of such secondary effects, including creation and reinforcement of illicit markets in desired but proscribed goods and services, questionable distribution of limited police resources, invitation to police corruption, and other effects on police behavior and attitudes.[20]

Few formulations of the labeling school are absolutely unique to it or even startlingly new to sociology. Rather, this school serves to reorient some research on deviance in certain directions that had been unwisely neglected. Far from being in opposition to more traditional orientations, the labeling perspective tends to complement them by focusing on aspects of deviance and control that they have slighted or by approaching aspects that they have treated from somewhat different angles. With this point in mind, let us turn now to the relations between labeling analysis and certain other theoretical orientations. As we shall see, even though the prospects for a single comprehensive and unified theory of deviance and control are uncertain, the elements of convergence between the labeling and other perspectives are considerable.

[20] See Edwin M. Schur, *Crimes Without Victims* (Englewood Cliffs, N.J.: Prentice-Hall, 1965); see also Herbert L. Packer, *The Limits of the Criminal Sanction* (Palo Alto: Stanford University Press, 1968).

six

Theoretical convergences

The phenomenological cast

As we have seen, the labeling approach has close affinities with symbolic interactionism, both in specific research methods and in general scientific aims. Some contemporary sociologists of deviance have tried to go one step farther in developing what may be called a "microsociology of meaning," drawing on some of the perspectives of phenomenological philosophy. This move is not very surprising, given the current considerable disenchantment with a narrow empiricism and the desire to forge a sociology geared to more general understanding. Indeed, as Severyn Bruyn has pointed out, "The interests of the phenomenologist and the participant observer are remarkably similar, although phenomenology never developed in the United States as it did in Europe."[1]

Renewed attention in current American sociology to the sub-

---

[1] Severyn Bruyn, *The Human Perspective in Sociology* (Englewood Cliffs, N.J.: Prentice-Hall, 1966), pp. 90–91.

jective sources of individual action has been accompanied by increased reference to phenomenological concepts, particularly as they have been set forth by the sociologist-philosopher Alfred Schutz, whose work has also been drawn upon heavily and applied by Harold Garfinkel (under the rubric "ethnomethodology").[2] Because of the relatively sudden spurt of interest in such perspectives, the rather ponderous terminology involved, and the apparent overriding influence of Garfinkel's work in this area, ethnomethodology has understandably elicited charges of faddism and cultism.[3] Yet just as it is intellectually naïve to assume that a new terminology necessarily indicates a new theoretical framework, it is gratuitously cynical to dismiss this perspective as only a fad without having considered its substance and potential contribution. It is not possible to attempt here any exploration in depth of the strictly philosophical premises and ramifications of phenomenology. Yet a brief look at its potential applications to sociology, especially to the sociology of deviance, should have value.

CENTRAL TENETS

A basic theme, emphasized over and over again in phenomenological writings, is the need to return "to the things themselves," as Edmund Husserl expressed it.[4] The world must somehow be recognized as it is directly experienced by human actors and not through the application of imposed concepts. Peter Berger and Thomas Luckmann have recently described this aim:

> The theoretical formulations of reality, whether they be scientific or philosophical or even mythological, do not exhaust what is "real" for the members of a society. Since this is so, the

2 Alfred Schutz, *The Phenomenology of the Social World*, trans. by G. Walsh and F. Lehnert (Evanston, Ill.: Northeastern University Press, 1967); and Schutz, *Collected Papers* (3 vols.; the Hague: Nijhoff, 1964, 1966, 1967); and Harold Garfinkel, *Studies in Ethnomethodology* (Englewood Cliffs, N.J.: Prentice-Hall, 1967).

3 See the review symposium on Garfinkel's *Studies in Ethnomethodology* in *American Sociological Review*, 33 (February 1968), 122–130.

4 Edmund Husserl, *Ideas*, trans. by W. R. Boyce Gibson (New York: Collier Books, 1962), pp. 37–88.

sociology of knowledge must first of all concern itself with what people "know" as "reality" in their everyday, non- or pre-theoretical lives. In other words, commonsense "knowledge" rather than "ideas" must be the central focus for the sociology of knowledge. It is precisely this "knowledge" that constitutes the fabric of meaning without which no society could exist.[5]

Social science itself, even as it seeks to understand human life, must be recognized as typically applying an overlay of secondary constructs, rather than as simply invoking direct apprehension of experience. As Maurice Merleau-Ponty has declared:

> The whole universe of science is built upon the world as directly experienced, and if we want to subject science itself to rigorous scrutiny and arrive at a precise assessment of its meaning and scope, we must begin by reawakening the basic experience of the world of which science is the second-order expression. . . . To return to things themselves is to return to that world which precedes knowledge, of which knowledge always *speaks*, and in relation to which every scientific schematization is an abstract and derivative sign-language, as is geography in relation to the countryside in which we have learnt beforehand what a forest, a prairie or a river is.[6]

A narrow empiricism geared to testing causal hypotheses and establishing statistical regularities is considered inadequate if the social sciences are to achieve this goal. It is claimed that the emphasis should be placed instead on developing intimate understanding of the subjective meanings of human action through techniques of intensive observation, detailed description, even "intuition." Social science, according to Schutz, "sets as its primary goal the greatest possible clarification of what is thought about the social world by those living in it."[7] This apparently free-wheeling subjectivism does not imply abandonment of empiricism, its pro-

---

[5] Peter L. Berger and Thomas Luckmann, *The Social Construction of Reality* (Garden City, N.Y.: Doubleday, 1966), p. 14.

[6] Maurice Merleau-Ponty, "What is Phenomenology?" from *Phenomenology of Perception* (1962), in Joseph J. Kockelmans, ed., *Phenomenology* (Garden City, N.Y.: Doubleday Anchor, 1967), pp. 358–359.

[7] Schutz, *The Phenomenology of the Social World*, p. 222.

ponents insist. Rather it aims at an even broader basis in the real "facts" of human experience, although the techniques for establishing it are not all "scientific" in the most rigorously technical sense. One writer has even argued that phenomenology "goes beyond positive science by aiming at absolute certainty for its foundations and at freedom from presuppositions that have not passed phenomenological scrutiny."[8] Sociologist Edward Tiryakian has suggested that a phenomenological orientation can usually complement positivist research and that it seems to aim at "trans-objectivity," at an explanation that "goes beyond the object to a complex elucidation of the multiple perspectives and the social spatial-temporal dimensions of the social phenomenon."[9]

Phenomenologically oriented analysts stress the reflexive and dialectical features of the social world. At the root of the endeavor lies a radical opposition to the conception of a dichotomy between subject and object. As the existential psychiatrist Rollo May, writing in the same general intellectual tradition as that of the phenomenologists, has commented:

> . . . the person and his world are a unitary, structural whole; the hyphenation of the phrase being-in-the-world expresses precisely that. The two poles, self and world, are always dialectically related. Self implies world and world self; there is neither without the other, and each is understandable only in terms of the other.[10]

The concept of "intentionality," the phenomenological claim that consciousness is always "consciousness of" something, finds its sociological counterpart in an insistence upon the reflexive nature of meaning and of social facts themselves. Garfinkel provided an early statement of this view in a discussion of Schutz's work:

> Rather than there being a world of concrete objects which a theory cuts this way and that, the view holds that the cake is

8 Herbert Spiegelberg, "Husserl's Phenomenology and Sartre's Existentialism," in Joseph J. Kockelmans, ed., *Phenomenology* (Garden City, N.Y.: Doubleday Anchor, 1967), p. 253.

9 Edward A. Tiryakian, "Existential Phenomenology and the Sociological Tradition," *American Sociological Review*, 30 (October 1965), 687.

10 Rollo May, "Contributions of Existential Psychotherapy," in May, ed., *Existence* (New York: Simon & Schuster, 1967), p. 59

constituted in the very act of cutting. No cutting, no cake, there being no reality out there that is approximated since the world in this view is as it appears.[11]

More recently Berger and Luckmann have insisted that

> the objectivity of the institutional world, however massive it may appear to the individual, is a humanly produced, constructed objectivity . . . the relationship between man, the producer, and the social world, his product, is and remains a dialectical one. That is, man (not, of course, in isolation but in his collectivities) and his social world interact with each other. The product acts back upon the producer.[12]

Social reality, then, is constructed, or, as Garfinkel has often put it, social facts should be viewed as an "accomplishment."

Space, time, and affectivity are important concerns for the phenomenological sociologist. Space and time have their socially constructed, meaningful aspects and are inadequately represented solely in terms of conventional measurable physical dimensions. (The attention to space ties in well with the interests of symbolic interactionists, particularly their concern with gesture and non-verbal communication.) Schutz has developed a scheme for viewing human action within a framework of diverse "dimensions of the social world," relating the actor to a host of relevant contemporaries, predecessors, and potential successors.[13] Whereas actors in face-to-face relationships may govern their behavior by processes of direct "intersubjective understanding," more complex and indirect means of framing ideal types ("typification") are called into play to deal with people with whom one does not have direct contact. But the important point is that these several kinds of relationships—direct and indirect, as well as present, past, and future —may all influence continuing social action and our understanding of the social world.

An orientation to the future seems especially pronounced in

11 Garfinkel, "The Perception of the Other: A Study in Social Order" (Unpublished doctoral dissertation, Harvard University, 1952), pp. 95–96.
12 Berger and Luckmann, *op. cit.*, p. 57.
13 Schutz, *The Phenomenology of the Social World*, pp. 139–214.

phenomenological analysis. Schutz has written of the processes of social action:

> All projecting consists in anticipation of future conduct by way of phantasying, yet it is not the ongoing process of action but the phantasied act as having been accomplished which is the starting point of all projecting. I have to visualize the state of affairs to be brought about by my future action before I can draft the single steps of such future acting from which this state of affairs will result. Metaphorically speaking, I must have some idea of the structure to be erected before I can draft the blueprints. Thus I have to place myself in my phantasy at a future time, when this action *will* already *have been* accomplished.[14]

This "future perfect tense," as Schutz has called it, is, of course, highly reminiscent of "taking the role of the other" and "projecting courses of action," emphasized by symbolic interactionists. Indeed, Schutz has quite explicitly acknowledged his general indebtedness to George Mead, an indebtedness that is perhaps especially apparent on this point.

A similar emphasis is noticeable in the concept of *Dasein* developed by existential psychiatry. As May has stated,

> *Dasein* indicates that man is the being who *is there* and implies also that he *has* a "there" in the sense that he can know he is there and can take a stand with reference to that fact. . . . Man is the being who can be conscious of, and therefore responsible for, his existence.

May has also suggested that to American readers the term "becoming" may most vividly capture the gist of *Dasein* and that, for the existential analyst, the future is

> the dominant mode of time for human beings. Personality can be understood only as we see it on a trajectory toward its future; a man can understand himself only as he projects himself forward. This is a corollary of the fact that the person is always becoming, always emerging into the future.[15]

14 *Ibid.*, p. 20.
15 May, *op. cit.*, pp. 41, 68–69.

Affect is also central to any phenomenological approach to social life. Tiryakian has noted that a major theme of the existentialist-phenomenological tradition has been

> that human existence is disclosed in affective states: our existential self (*Dasein*) is always a sentient self (even indifference is a feeling), and the structure of our orientation to our situation is a spatial-temporal one of emotiveness.

Noting Max Scheler's important work exploring "the effective nature of experience by suggesting the interdependence between affect and social structure (i.e., social bonds and roles have an affective structural basis reflected in personality)," Tiryakian has suggested that recent sociology has tended to neglect this important area.[16] Clearly, if the major goal is to understand how the social world is experienced by the actors that populate it, feelings as well as beliefs or ideas, come very much to the fore. We thus find in the work of Goffman and Garfinkel, influenced by both phenomenology and symbolic interactionism, that such affective states as indignation, fear, humiliation, shame, and embarrassment have become major focal points for analysis. The interest of such sociologists in gestures and other nonverbal communication and in linguistic usage is partly related to this effort to capture the affective component in social situations.

Another important theme stressed by existentialists and phenomenologists is that of freedom and personal responsibility. This emphasis, too, is to some extent shared with the symbolic interactionists: Man is not simply a passive object on which external forces exert their influence but rather an active, reflecting force in shaping his own experience and that of others with whom he interacts. After noting the importance of voluntarism in the early work of Talcott Parsons and suggesting that such a notion is central to any real theory of social action, Tiryakian has claimed that it has been cast aside in recent years under the influence of Freudian and positivist concepts.[17] As we shall see, recent soci-

16 Tiryakian, *op. cit.*, p. 677.
17 *Ibid.*, pp. 684–686; see also Bruyn, *op. cit.*, pp. 43–50.

ologists (especially some working in the field of deviance) have picked up the theme of responsibility and stressed its importance in social analysis, even, in some instances, to the extent of building it into the very definition of deviance. But a balanced consideration of deterministic forces and personal responsibilities for social behavior is still uncertain. Although followers of this tradition usefully insist that notions of responsibility cannot be ignored, it does not follow that the tradition provides or directly leads to clear-cut guidelines for social and legal policies in areas in which individual responsibility becomes a public issue.

A final general point is the insistence of the phenomenological sociologist that thoroughgoing analysis of constructed meanings be applied not only to the observed social world but also to the operations of the observing sociologist himself. Science itself, as already noted, is considered an order of secondary constructs; the sociologist, therefore, is constructing reality through his research work, and his creation and use of concepts, classifications, and techniques must be scrutinized in order to understand the patterns of social life that he "finds." The editor of a recent phenomenologically oriented book on deviance has written of "the positivist practice of substituting phenomena of their own construction for those of common-sense, everyday life and then studying their own ad hoc phenomena as if these constituted 'reality.' "[18]

The phenomenological analysis of sociological operations has been a central concern of "ethnomethodology," as represented by Garfinkel's work. In a sense, this attention to the sociologist's construction of meanings is a counterpart to the concern of the labeling school with the impact of organizational imperatives upon the processing of deviants. The necessity for the sociological research team to produce an acceptable "account" (to use a term often adopted by ethnomethodologists) of its operations is very much like the necessity for the blindness organization to maintain itself as a going concern. The results are similar too. The "findings"

18 Jack D. Douglas, "Deviance and Respectability: The Social Construction of Moral Meanings," in Douglas, ed., *Deviance and Respectability* (New York: Basic Books, 1970), p. 8.

emanating from sociological research and analysis operations constitute a socially constructed "accomplishment" (another term that Garfinkel uses frequently). The nature and experience of the blind population are also to some extent the "accomplishment" of programs shaped by organizational needs. This point has been made strongly by Garfinkel in analyzing the operations of an outpatient psychiatric clinic. After finding that "ad hoc considerations are essential features of coding procedures," he has gone on to suggest the possibility that

> . . . the coded results consist of a persuasive version of the socially organized character of the clinic's operations, regardless of what the actual order is, perhaps independently of what the actual order is, and even without the investigator having detected the actual order. Instead of our study of patients' clinic careers (as well as the multitude of studies of various social arrangements that have been carried out in similarly conventional ways) having described the order of the clinic's operations, the account may be argued to consist of a socially invented, persuasive, and proper way of talking about the clinic as an orderly enterprise, since "after all" the account was produced by "scientific producers."[19]

PHENOMENOLOGY AND DEVIANCE

Although the perspectives of phenomenology, or ethnomethodology, could well be applied to the analysis of any or all aspects of the social world (indeed, the proponents of this orientation consider it an all-embracing yet distinct way of viewing human experience and social life generally), deviance and control have been of special interest to analysts working in this tradition recently. We may speculate as to why. Some factors discussed earlier as contributions to the growing interest in labeling processes may also promote the phenomenological approach. In particular, disenchantment with conventional quantitative approaches and the feeling that the "findings" from such research have been superficial and relatively useless—that they have failed to provide any

[19] Garfinkel, *Studies in Ethnomethodology*, p. 23.

real sense of how people experience deviance situations—make the phenomenological orientation seem very attractive to analysts of deviance. Seriously deviating behavior appears, at least to some sociologists, as especially difficult to explain on the basis of any kind of consensus-oriented structuralism, for an understanding of this kind of behavior an attempt to gain access to the subjective meanings involved seems particularly important. That some deviations seem to challenge accepted ways of viewing "reality" may also encourage sociologists to attempt a radical stripping away of secondary classifications and conceptions to bare the meaning of "the things themselves."

Also contributing to the relatively strong interest of phenomenologists in deviance is the notion—well developed by Garfinkel and his followers—that analysis of deviance is a major methodological device for understanding social order. This point is, of course, one that has been recognized by various sociologists in the past (Émile Durkheim's *Suicide* may be considered a prime example), but it has been operationalized in an interesting way by the ethnomethodologists. Garfinkel's studies of the "routine grounds of everyday activities" have provided the best illustration of the research "use" of deviation. His aim has been well stated:

> Procedurally it is my preference to start with familiar scenes and ask what can be done to make trouble. The operations that one would have to perform in order to multiply the senseless features of perceived environments; to produce and sustain bewilderment, consternation, and confusion; to produce the socially structured affects of anxiety, shame, guilt, and indignation; and to produce disorganized interaction should tell us something about how the structures of everyday activities are ordinarily and routinely produced and maintained.[20]

Through such techniques, Garfinkel has insisted, it may be possible to uncover the "background expectancies" that are usually taken for granted or remain unnoticed but that the individual uses as a "scheme of interpretation" to guide his interaction in ordinary

[20] *Ibid.*, pp. 37–38.

social situations. As Tiryakian has noted, this research procedure can be considered a kind of sociological counterpart of the "bracketing" of derivative and secondary aspects that the phenomenologist thinks necessary for the "reduction" of the observed world to its basic phenomena.[21]

A final reason for the special attention of this school to matters of deviance arises from the sociologist's moral concerns. The widespread reevaluation of norms and values in modern society has helped to bring the topics of deviance and control to the forefront of sociological research and analysis. And phenomenology and existentialism, with their emphasis on voluntarism, their special focus on issues of freedom and responsibility, and their long concern with what is sometimes described as "the moral crisis of modern society,"[22] seem to provide an especially appropriate intellectual framework.

At any rate, quite a few specific studies of deviance and control are now being undertaken from a phenomenological perspective or at least employ phenomenological (or ethnomethodological) terminology. Some of the research on law-enforcement processes discussed earlier falls into this category. David Sudnow's study of the office of public defender, in which he has viewed the creation and use by attorneys of a classification of "normal crimes" as a form of "typification," is explicitly in this tradition. Egon Bittner, in his study of the policing of Skid Row, has also relied on the (ethnomethodological) approach of intensive observation and description of practical, everyday activities to produce a picture of the police's "peace-keeping" work as a skilled accomplishment.

Aaron Cicourel's analysis of the "social organization of juvenile justice" is even more directly grounded in phenomenological concepts, and Cicourel has explicitly acknowledged his indebtedness to phenomenological theory. We have already noted his insistence on the inadequacy of official delinquency records and on the need to observe directly the relevant interactions (like those

21 Tiryakian, *op. cit.*, p. 678, n.23; on the matter of reduction, see the several statements reproduced in Kockelmans, *op. cit.*, pp. 58–79.
22 Tiryakian, *Sociologism and Existentialism* (Englewood Cliffs, N.J.: Prentice-Hall, 1962).

between youths and probation officers) in order to grasp the social construction of definitions:

> The problems of objectification and verification cannot be resolved by appeals to technical skills in capturing or "bottling" the phenomena invoked as observational sources of data. The sociologist must come to grips with the problem of making the background expectancies visible. . . .[23]

Through such intensive observation and analysis of direct interaction, Cicourel has revealed the significance of processing contingencies and of negotiation and retrospective interpretation; he has also highlighted the ways in which the behavior of juvenile-court personnel reflects their efforts to make sense of the patterns of behavior and types of individuals with which they must deal. Cicourel's indebtedness to the phenomenological tradition is especially clear in his concluding comment, in which he expresses the desire to "bracket" even the secondary scientific constructs that have guided most sociological research on deviance:

> The contrasting view followed in this book is to view the assembly of a product (for example, a statistic, a juvenile labeled "delinquent"), recognized by societal members as "routine" and called the "social structures" by sociologists, as being generated by practical decision-making. . . . The present work has sought to avoid a search for "underlying" ideals by seeking to discover those thoughts and taken-for-granted elements participants of conversations and documents utilize for producing utterances and making decisions they routinely honor as "communication." Consequently, how members "fill in" equivocal utterances to "close" their meaning, state they "know what you mean," assume they "see the point," has been the central concern of the present study. . . .[24]

Perhaps not surprisingly, the types of deviation that have lent themselves most readily to phenomenological analysis are those that are otherwise particularly elusive and seemingly "interior," like sui-

---

[23] Aaron V. Cicourel, *The Social Organization of Juvenile Justice* (New York: Wiley, 1968), p. 15.
[24] *Ibid.*, pp. 332–333.

cide and mental illness. In his effort to develop this perspective, Jack Douglas has concluded that the practical application of even such an apparently unequivocal definition of behavior as that of suicide is subject to negotiation, that suicidal outcomes are indeed socially constructed accomplishments. Douglas has concentrated on the "situated meanings" of suicidal acts for the individuals involved and for those who must react to such acts. If we really wish to tap such meanings, statistical comparisons do not seem fully adequate. Such comparisons have tended, as Douglas has remarked, to slight both the situational contexts of specific suicidal acts and the elements of intention in individual suicides. Douglas has argued that, rather than attempting to understand individual instances in terms of generalizations developed through statistically based comparisons and classifications, we should start from detailed examination of specific cases:

> We propose to study human actions and their "meanings" from the bottom upward, at least in some good part. . . . The *ideal* of this approach is to go from what people say and do in the real world situations upward toward an analysis of the patterns that can be found in their actions and the meanings of their statements and behavior; then, only when the problems of these levels of investigation have been solved, to proceed to develop theories of the social meanings.[25]

This method implies very close and serious attention to such "data" as suicide notes, conversations before suicide, and the events and situations that constitute the social context of particular suicidal acts. After claiming that suicides in our culture are meaningful (in the sense that they are susceptible to explanation) and intentional (in that the victims are usually presumed to have intended to die), Douglas has suggested that individuals who commit suicide can sometimes be viewed as having attempted to tell others something about their "selves." Another very real possibility is that suicidal action may be used against others as a kind of indirect revenge, to engender guilt and the like. In his argument

25 Douglas, *The Social Meanings of Suicide* (Princeton: Princeton University Press, 1967), p. 256.

that the individual's use of suicide to "blame" others for his death is "a common intended meaning of suicidal actions," Douglas has remarked the difficulty presented to survivors by such behavior, apparent in direct or indirect accusation in suicide notes, and the ways in which this difficulty may be a potent factor in shaping the "labeling" of suicides:

> . . . those who are blamed have a difficult time trying to define things in a way more acceptable to themselves. . . . They would seem to have only two courses of action that promise exoneration: that of redefining what happened (it wasn't "really" the way he said it was) . . . and that of redefining the person who committed the suicidal action—he was "crazy" or he was just trying to harm us. . . . This might well help to explain why it is that so many individuals who attempt suicidal actions are treated as "crazy" (sent to psychiatrists, etc.) by their significant others and why individuals who intend their suicidal actions to blame others often use less direct means of blaming (i.e., so that they won't be clearly *just* "aggressive").[26]

Douglas has noted the complex (and sometimes circular) labeling processes that may be reflected in this tendency to define suicidal actions as indicative of mental disturbance. Just as suicide threat or attempt may be a major reason why an individual is defined as mentally ill, so the very definition of mental illness may strongly convey to the individual the assurance that he is the kind of person who might kill himself, an assurance that clearly may function as a potent self-fulfilling prophecy. There is thus for the psychotherapist

> a patterned conflict between the obligations and expectations that a specialist is subject to in this situation: suicidal phenomena are seen as relevant considerations, they are seen as important to the whole therapeutic relationship and process, and yet the therapist must avoid giving suicidal thoughts to the patient.[27]

One of the most impressive efforts to apply phenomenolgical perspectives to the analysis of deviation—and one that until re-

26 *Ibid.*, p. 314.
27 *Ibid.*, pp. 330, 331.

cently was rather badly neglected by sociologists—can be found among the writings of the "existential psychiatrists." In introducing a collection of essays on existential psychiatry, Rollo May has posed the following central question:

> Can we be sure . . . that we are seeing the patient as he really is, knowing him in his own reality; or are we seeing merely a projection of our own theories *about* him? . . . the crucial question is always the bridge between the system and the patient—how can we be certain that our system, admirable and beautifully wrought as it may be in principle, has anything whatever to do with this specific Mr. Jones, a living, immediate reality sitting opposite us in the consulting room? May not just this particular person require another system, another quite different frame of reference? And does not this patient, or any person for that matter, evade our investigations, slip through our scientific fingers like seafoam, precisely to the extent that we rely on the logical consistency of our own system?[28]

The British psychiatrist R. D. Laing has emphasized precisely the same problem, asking, "How can I go straight to the patients if the psychiatric words at my disposal keep the patient at a distance from me?"[29] Objective theory and technical classification, must, then, according to this school, be subordinated to the immediate reality of the human being and his unique experience and perceptions. Far from standing apart and assessing the patient in a disinterested way, the therapist must involve himself, must indeed attempt to enter into the other's experience, if he is really to understand him. As both May and Laing have emphasized, true objectivity does not require (indeed is blocked by) depersonalization of the patient, treatment of him as an object. "The world of this particular patient must be grasped from the inside, be known and seen so far as possible from the angle of the one who exists in it."[30] Earlier we referred to the orientation of existential psychiatry toward the future; the existential analyst resists the

28 May, *op. cit.*, p. 3.
29 R. D. Laing, *The Divided Self* (Baltimore: Penguin, 1965), p. 18.
30 May, *op. cit.*, p. 56.

tendency of orthodox psychoanalysis to stress overwhelmingly the deterministic influences of early childhood relations and events. The past may indeed have importance, but if one is to come to grips with the individual human being-in-the-world he must not "evade the immediate, anxiety-creating issues in the present by taking refuge behind the determinism of the past."[31]

A radical attempt to understand why the patient's fantasies, delusions, and dreams are as they are in the light of his own experience, his personal existence, is required. May has noted that the focus of existential psychiatry in the analysis of dreams is on what a patient's dream says

> about *where* he is at the moment and what he is moving toward. . . . The context is the patient not as a set of psychic dynamisms or mechanisms but as a human being who is choosing, committing, and pointing himself toward something right now; the context is dynamic, immediately real and present.[32]

By stripping away all formal conceptual apparatus and, of course, any vestiges of "passing judgment" on the patient, as well as by attending closely to the ways in which a patient describes his experience, the existential psychiatrist may achieve much greater understanding of the subjective meaning of even a severe disorder than had earlier been considered possible. When the existential analysts claim that "the mentally ill live in 'worlds' different from ours,"[33] they are stressing that, no matter how disordered or incomprehensible such "worlds" may seem to the outsider, they are very real to the individuals experiencing them; and, of course, they are also very real sociologically, for they have definite effects upon social behavior and situations. Laing has taken an even more radical step, asking in effect whether or not those individuals whom we consider "normal" are necessarily always "saner" than are those whom we label "mentally ill." "The statesmen of the world who boast and threaten that they have Doomsday weapons

31 *Ibid.,* p. 70.
32 *Ibid.,* p. 77.
33 Ludwig Binswanger, "The Existential Analysis School of Thought," in May, ed., *Existence* (New York: Simon & Schuster, 1952), p. 213.

are far more dangerous, and far more estranged from 'reality' than many of the people on whom the label 'psychotic' is affixed."[34]

Recently a few sociologists have analyzed mental illness and related issues within a framework similar to or influenced by that of the phenomenologists. Thomas Scheff, in his study of the negotiation aspects of psychiatric diagnosis and in his more ambitious development of a general sociological theory of mental illness,[35] has drawn upon some of the concepts and perspectives of this school, particularly the socially constructed nature of what we call "mental illness." Alan Blum, drawing upon linguistic research into the meaning of verdicts of "not guilty by reason of insanity" in criminal trials, has emphasized the need to concentrate on the processes through which such definitions are "produced."[36] It is not enough merely to cite the labeling process involved; we must also attempt to describe in detail just what it consists of.

CONTRIBUTIONS AND LIMITATIONS

Although some sociologists who consider their work to be ethnomethodological seem to believe that the approach represents a radical break with traditional sociology, it should be clear from the preceding discussion that this claim is at the very least an exaggeration. When we combine the conceptual framework of Mead's symbolic interactionism with Max Weber's insistence that sociology must attend to subjective meanings and produce explanations that are meaningfully as well as causally adequate (Schutz has clearly acknowledged his great indebtedness to both Weber and Mead), we bring together most of the key elements in the phenomenological approach to social action. As we shall see, ethnomethodological work sharpens the focus on some relevant matters

[34] Laing, *op. cit.*, p. 12.
[35] Thomas J. Scheff, "Negotiating Reality: Notes on Power in the Assessment of Responsibility," *Social Problems*, 16 (Summer 1968), 3–17; and Scheff, *Being Mentally Ill* (Chicago: Aldine, 1966).
[36] Alan F. Blum, "The Sociology of Mental Illness," in Douglas, ed., *Deviance and Respectability* (New York: Basic Books, 1970), pp. 31–60.

and pushes certain lines of exploration to a point that might not be achieved by more conventional sociology, but otherwise the approach hardly qualifies as new. Nor is the claim of some phenomenologically oriented analysts of deviance, that ethnomethodology begins where a labeling approach ends,[37] very persuasive.

Our review of some of the specific research conducted by such sociologists indicates that they have a great deal in common with analysts of the labeling school, as well as with others working in the tradition of symbolic interactionism. Among the important common elements in this work are, first, the basic premise that "deviance" is a socially constructed category; second, the consequent primary focus on societal reactions, rather than on the characteristics of, or other precipitating factors influencing, the deviating individual; third, the attempt to approach an understanding of deviance from the point of view of the deviator, rather than from that of "respectables" and official control agents; fourth, heavy reliance on the concept "definition of the situation" and recognition that such definition is to some extent "negotiated"; and, fifth, intensive observation as a research technique.

The work of ethnomethodologists has served to heighten the emphasis on certain of these same common themes, as well as to introduce a few additional and more distinctive ones. In the sociology of deviance, four themes appear to highlight the most useful aspects of the phenomenological scheme.

Insistence on distinguishing the social and natural sciences
The sharp distinction between social and natural sciences is implicit in many of the features that we have mentioned: in the emphasis on subjective meanings as a key element in social action; in the concern with actors' common-sense knowledge of everyday life; in the expressed preference for methods geared to *verstehen*, or general understanding; and in the view of social science as an order of secondary constructs. Schutz has commented:

> . . . a theory which aims at explaining social reality has to develop particular devices foreign to the natural sciences in order

---

37 See for example Douglas, "Deviance and Respectability."

to agree with the common-sense experience of the social world . . . the observational field of the social scientist—social reality —has a specific meaning and relevance structure for the human beings living, acting, and thinking within it. . . . The thought objects constructed by the social scientist, in order to grasp this social reality, have to be founded upon the thought objects constructed by the common-sense thinking of men, living their daily life within their social world. Thus, the constructs of the social sciences are, so to speak, constructs of the second degree, that is, constructs of the constructs made by the actors on the social scene, whose behavior the social scientist has to observe and to explain in accordance with the procedural rules of his science.[38]

The distinctive approach required for the social sciences is often used by phenomenologists as a counter balance to the philosophy and method of behaviorism. Behaviorists, they argue, believe that adequate explanations can be derived from investigation of externally observable and measurable behavior. According to phenomenologists, this approach reduces man to the status of inert object and thus fails to take into account the subjective aspects of human social action. There is, however, some irony in the fact that, despite this antibehaviorist stance and this stress on subjective meanings, the detailed ethnographic method relied on by the ethnomethodologists sometimes seems to elevate the minutiae of externally observed behavior to a central place in analysis.[39] The rejoinder that such detailed descriptions provide better bases for inferring relevant meaning structures than do conventional survey methods does not entirely answer this objection. At any rate, the phenomenologist's focus on the "human" aspects of social situations is valuable by and large. In deviance analysis more specifically, insistence that the methods of natural science are not fully appropriate to the object matter of the social sciences is consistent with renewed interest in studying deviation and control through nonquantitative research techniques.

Microscopic analysis of interaction processes in reaction to deviation   As we have seen, a broadly based labeling approach to

[38] Schutz, *Collected Papers*, pp. 58–59.
[39] See, for example, Sherri Cavan, *Liquor License* (Chicago: Aldine, 1966).

the study of deviance includes analysis at a number of levels and goes considerably beyond social-psychological concentration on face-to-face interaction. Ethnomethodologists, on the other hand, have tended to focus on this latter level of analysis and to dissect the processes found there including language, as well as gesture and other nonverbal communication, as key indicators of meaning, in an extremely thorough and intensive way. The ingenious efforts by Harold Garfinkel and Peter McHugh[40] to develop methodologies designed to uncover background expectancies and to explain as fully as possible just how people go about formulating "definitions of the situation" have perhaps been particularly noteworthy. The value of ethnomethodological work has also been very significant in exploring what we might call "interpersonal," rather than social, deviance. Breaches of etiquette, violations of interpersonal trust, and similar small-scale deviations from the norms that guide interpersonal relations are not only interesting sociologically in themselves, but may also provide a microcosmic basis for analyzing deviance situations in general.[41]

Stress on individual integrity and antideterminism   Whereas both symbolic interactionists and phenomenologists view man as an active agent who chooses among alternatives, the phenomenologists appear to give special attention to this matter. Emphasis on human purpose and freedom is closely tied to the claim that distinctive methods are necessary in the social sciences. In the belief that what modern social science has done "is banish human *purpose* from its universe of discourse," Charles Hampden-Turner has recently argued for "a new philosophy for the social sciences—a complete reassessment of what a science of humanity should be . . . a total reversal of the mechanistic, reactive, and physicalist treatment of man."[42] We shall return in a later section to the thorny issue of personal responsibility for deviating acts. By em-

---

40 Peter McHugh, *Defining the Situation* (Indianapolis: Bobbs-Merrill, 1968).

41 See Norman K. Denzin, "Rules of Conduct and the Study of Deviant Behavior: Some Notes on the Social Relationship," in Douglas, ed., *Deviance and Respectability* (New York: Basic Books, 1970), p. 120–159.

42 Charles Hampden-Turner, *Radical Man* (Cambridge, Mass.: Schenkman, 1970), pp. 10, 14.

phasizing human freedom and choice analysts working in the existential-phenomenological tradition have at least challenged complacent acceptance of the typical determinist "explanations" of deviance.

Analysis of the operations of sociology itself   Whereas conventional sociologists have been well aware of such methodological problems as coder reliability and effects of interviewers on the course of an interview, the ethnomethodologists have gone farther and insisted on radical scrutiny of the ways in which sociologists construct "reality" during their research and analysis. In the study of deviance, for example, it is almost impossible to conduct research without oneself engaging in some kinds of indirect "labeling." But just how far the sociologist can afford to go in casting aside the concepts and classifications developed through past research and theorizing is not clear. Although it is important to confront the living reality of the particular individual or situation under investigation, the social scientist nevertheless seeks to do more than describe discrete cases.

This statement should suggest the general methodological problem that plagues those who wish to apply phenomenological perspectives in sociology. Although the ethnomethodologists can produce many suggestive insights into deviation and control processes, their approach almost by definition will be weak in the production of systematic findings and in methods for systematically validating the hypotheses that it generates. We simply do not at present have definitive methods for systematically studying "meaning structures." We may recognize the importance of "intersubjective understanding" in human social action, but this recognition may well constitute more of a stumbling block to the social scientist than a guideline for his analysis. Although Schutz and others have argued vigorously that recognizing the unique features of each social situation and of a particular individual's subjective experience of a situation in no way requires us to abandon the goal of generalizing about social life, their arguments are not really persuasive. A phenomenological approach may save us from superficial "findings," but it may present us instead with perceptive "case studies" of discrete situations, on the basis of which it is difficult, if not impossible, to generalize and produce a systematic analysis of social patterns. Some analyses by existential psychiatrists may thus hold up well mainly as psychiatry, of which the goal is therapeutic: to understand and help *particular patients*. We need only read such classics of existential analysis as "The Case of Ellen West"[43] to appreciate how dependent the analyst is upon the perceptiveness and expressive skills of his patient. In a sense, the traditional aim of the social scientist, to devise methods for gaining "control over his data," has been turned around in existential analysis, in which the "quality" of the subject may largely determine how impressive the "findings" are.

These comments should not be taken as a denial of the contribution made by the phenomenological orientation to the study of deviance. It has produced some highly suggestive ideas, and, even though some of its proponents have exaggerated its distinctiveness, it has lent an interesting cast to recent research on deviance and control. It may be that, through its development of sophisticated ideal-typical explanations, it will lead the way in bridging the apparent gap between unrelated depth studies and systematic (statistical) findings. Although some ethnomethodologists insist that their approach is quite different from that of the labeling school, we have seen that actually the two are very similar. Indeed, even the relation between them, on one hand, and the structural-functional approach, on the other, is less problematic than some phenomenologists claim.

Functionalism and labeling

CRITICISMS OF FUNCTIONALISM

There are several reasons why labeling analysts and ethnomethodologists might be critical of structural-functional theory as it has been applied to problems of deviance and control. First, there has

[43] Binswanger, "The Case of Ellen West: An Anthropological-Clinical Study," in May, ed., *Existence* (New York: Simon & Schuster, 1952), pp. 237–364.

been a tendency in such functional analyses (of "anomie theory," "opportunity theory," and the like) to accept the official statistics on deviance as "given," to use them as a point of departure for explaining variations in rates of deviating behavior. Both the labeling and ethnomethodological approaches to deviance are grounded on the contrary premises that such official data are not valid representations of the actual distribution of deviation and that examination of such statistics will not enable us to answer the most important questions about deviance and control processes, experiences, and situations. There is still considerable controversy among sociologists of deviance over the actual distribution of deviating acts (for example, over the social-class distribution of delinquent behavior), but even those who tend to accept the general patterns revealed by official data as valid now acknowledge that such data do not provide a complete picture. The significance of the numerous contingencies that emerge in the course of specific social-control practices is being increasingly recognized.

A closely related objection to functional theories is that they are too rigidly deterministic. Calling for detailed examination of the "natural language" of the "practical activities" in delinquency-processing situations, Cicourel has declared:

> A question like "What forces motivate or structure the entrance into delinquent activity?" misses the general relevance of the problem of practical reasoning that juveniles engage in when pursuing daily activities, how the police and probation officials are drawn into contact with juveniles, and how the police or probation officers decide that particular events fall under general policies or rules deemed relevant. A simple reference to "forces" or "social structure" or "values" imposes an order instead of seeking to discover the nature of socially organized activities.[44]

It is one thing to demonstrate the existence and cultural transmission of a delinquent or other deviant "tradition" in certain neighborhoods or social categories; it is another to assume inexorable pressure on the individuals involved to engage in the

[44] Cicourel, *op. cit.*, pp. 168–169.

subculturally accepted behavior. As David Matza has pointed out, many early approaches to the study of deviance adopted a logic of "contagion," in which "it came to be thought that human subjects, if properly placed and sufficiently exposed must 'catch' a deviation." Perhaps more realistically, we should proceed according to Matza's logic in discussing Becker's studies of marihuana use: ". . . it becomes apparent that anyone can become a marihuana user and that *no one* has to."[45] Of course, if we adopt this logic, we must find some way to continue to account for the rather persuasive evidence that individuals located differently in the social order run different risks of (have systematically varying probabilities of) engaging in the behavior in question.

According to a third objection, functional theories of deviance tend to rest on premises somewhat similar to those underlying a "medical model" of deviance. Becker has commented that functional analysts may

> look at a society, or some part of a society, and ask whether there are any processes going on in it that tend to reduce its stability. . . . They label such processes deviant or identify them as symptoms of social disorganization. They discriminate between those features of society which promote stability (and thus are "functional") and those which disrupt stability (and thus are "dysfunctional").

Decisions on which practices are functional and which are not are extremely elusive and in fact are reached through processes of political conflict. "The functional view of deviance, by ignoring the political aspect of the phenomenon, limits our understanding."[46]

CONTRIBUTIONS OF FUNCTIONALISM

Despite these possible objections, examination of various functional analyses of deviance reveals a number of important contributions that hold up well even when we adopt a labeling orientation.

45 David Matza, *Becoming Deviant* (Englewood Cliffs, N.J.: Prentice-Hall, 1969), pp. 102, 110.
46 Howard S. Becker, *Outsiders* (New York: Free Press, 1964), p. 7.

To begin with, we should emphasize that the basic tenets of functional analysis—the mutual interdependence of the various units of the social system, the necessity of examining any one part of the system in its relation to other parts, and the assumption that change in one part will have repercussions elsewhere in the system—should be quite unobjectionable to the labeling analyst. Furthermore, even those functional analyses most directly susceptible to the criticisms noted have helped to turn the sociology of deviance away from earlier "explanations" oriented toward individuals and toward modes of analysis that the adherent of labeling finds more acceptable. For example, Robert Merton's well-known essay "Social Structure and Anomie,"[47] in which he seems to have accepted official data on social-class variations in delinquency as a basis for his theoretical interpretation of deviance patterns, nevertheless shifted attention from the deviating individuals toward the social system itself. Albert Cohen's seminal *Delinquent Boys*,[48] though it may have somewhat exaggerated the constraining force of deviant subculture, also called attention to the salience of the stratification order (a point quite consistent with a labeling analysis).

Furthermore, the generation of controversy over the social-class distribution of "actual" deviation, which prompted research on the processing contingencies that might intervene between acts of deviation and the official recording of some of those acts, can be considered an indirect contribution of these functionalist studies to the development of the labeling approach. Finally, the kinds of sociocultural pressures that these functional theories set forth as generators of deviance can, as we shall see to some extent at least, in the next section, be aligned with labeling analysis—for example, precipitating or "feeding in" variables that partly determine the probabilities that particular categories of individuals will undergo specified labeling processes.

There is more to the functional approach to deviance, however, than these admittedly important attempts to frame general

47 Robert K. Merton, "Social Structure and Anomie," in Merton, *Social Theory and Social Structure* (rev. ed.; New York: Free Press, 1959), pp. 131–160.
48 Albert K. Cohen, *Delinquent Boys* (New York: Free Press, 1955).

theories. Two other applications of functionalism—in the analysis of latent functions served by particular forms of deviation and in the investigation of the functions of reactions to deviation—are even more closely tied to the labeling orientation. A major contribution of functionalism, the beginnings of which lay in Merton's essay, with its attention to culturally prescribed values and socially approved avenues for attaining them, is its exposure of the "evil-causes-evil fallacy" that plagued much earlier deviance analysis. Despite Becker's admonition on the latent "medical model" that might underlie a functional approach, functionalism did largely demolish the assumption that deviation invariably springs from individual pathology by showing "the steady persistence of sin or evil instead of simply exposing or condemning it."[49] As Matza properly noted, Kingsley Davis' analysis of prostitution and Daniel Bell's essay "Crime as an American Way of Life" are major efforts of this type.[50]

Before turning to specific studies, however, we shall mention a more general aspect of the functions of particular forms of deviation. We should not overlook the fact that deviation, beside having functional links with the social system of which it is part, may also be in various ways directly functional for the individuals engaging in it. We should allow neither our concern with sociocultural disjunctions that push people into deviating acts nor our concentration on the impact of negative labeling in producing deviant "careers" to obscure the fact that deviation often has very direct "payoffs" for the individuals engaging in it. Sometimes, of course, there are direct economic rewards (a fact upon which Merton has partly based his analysis of "illicit means"). Claude Brown has written in his autobiographical account of life in Harlem:

> I guess it was harder on the girls than it was on anybody. Dixie started tricking when she was thirteen. She was big for her age, and "nice" ladies used to point at her and say, "Oh, ain't that

[49] Matza, *op. cit.*, p. 33.
[50] Kingsley Davis, "The Sociology of Prostitution," *American Sociological Review*, 2 (October 1937), 746–755; and Daniel Bell, *The End of Ideology* (New York: Collier Books, 1961), pp. 127–150.

a shame." But it wasn't. The shame of it was that she had to do it or starve. When she got hip and went out there on the street and started turning tricks, she started eating and she stopped starving.[51]

Although such a statement could be construed as illustrating the "illicit means" theory, it actually seems to pose somewhat more starkly the possibility of direct economic need. To understand the behavior in question, it does not seem necessary to posit an abstract acceptance of common cultural goals or any conscious cognitive or intellectual "decision" to reject institutionalized and legitimate "means." We are dealing with very real economic incentives and payoffs. As John Lofland has commented somewhat more generally:

> If deviant acts are so frequently effective and, in the short term, rational, explaining their occurrence may be less a question of understanding why they sometimes occur than of understanding why they do not occur more often. After all, deviant acts are often in compliance with two of American civilization's most cherished values: short-term efficiency and short-term effectiveness.[52]

Of course, the direct payoffs from deviation are not always economic. Some acts of deviation (like homosexual acts), may be engaged in because of deep needs or inclinations or quite simply because they are pleasurable (like marihuana use). Still others may result from personal beliefs (political or religious "deviations") or situational decisions (obtaining an abortion). Indeed, both single rule-violating acts and deviant "roles" or "careers" may have positive attractions. As Cohen has pointed out, some deviance "may have the primary function of affirming, in the language of gesture and deed, that one is a certain kind of person."[53]

Functional analysis has gone beyond observation of such direct functions for the deviating individual to suggest as well the

[51] Claude Brown, *Manchild in the Promised Land* (New York: Signet, 1965), p. 169.

[52] John Lofland, *Deviance and Identity* (Englewood Cliffs, N.J.: Prentice-Hall, 1969), p. 54.

[53] Cohen, "The Sociology of the Deviant Act: Anomie Theory and Beyond," *American Sociological Review,* 30 (February 1965), 13.

links between certain specific patterns of deviation and the general social order. Davis has noted that prostitution, often considered pathological, actually shares with other sexual institutions in our kind of society a basic element, "the employment of sex for non-sexual ends within a competitive-authoritative system." Prostitution thus resembles major patterns of socially approved behavior: "It is one end of a long sequence or gradation of essentially similar phenomena that stretches at the other end to such approved patterns as engagement and marriage."[54] Although it is disapproved because the gratification involved is not tied to the basic social functions of procreation and socialization of the young, prostitution meets a genuine social demand and is not likely ever to vanish completely. On the other hand, according to Davis, "the particular form of institutionalization may change." He predicted what in fact has occurred since his article was written, a change toward greater sexual freedom that would inevitably affect prostitution because "the greater the proportion of free, mutually pleasurable intercourse, the lesser is the demand for prostitution. . . ." He then turned this analysis around in a striking way:

> If we reverse the proposition that increased sex freedom among women of all classes reduces the role of prostitution, we find ourselves admitting that increased prostitution may reduce the sexual irregularities of respectable women. This, in fact, has been the ancient justification for tolerated prostitution—that it "protected" the family and kept the wives and daughters of the respectable citizenry pure. . . . Such a view strikes us as paradoxical, because in popular discourse an evil such as prostitution cannot cause a good such as feminine virtue, or vice versa. Yet, as our analysis has implied throughout, there is a close connection between prostitution and the structure of the family.[55]

The discovery of latent functions of deviation, then, requires, as Merton has stressed, substituting objective social analysis for naïve moral judgment. In his analysis of the political machine

[54] Davis, *op. cit.*, p. 746.
[55] Davis, *op. cit.*, rev. ed. in Robert K. Merton and Robert A. Nisbet, eds., *Contemporary Social Problems* (New York: Harcourt Brace Jovanovich, 1961), pp. 283–284.

or boss system (often viewed simply as "bad" or "undesirable") he has noted that such structures persisted because they provided "an apparatus for satisfying otherwise unfulfilled needs of diverse groups in the population. . . ."[56] Similarly, Bell has found that certain kinds of criminal activity provided avenues of social mobility for certain groups to whom other avenues were not readily available.[57] And William F. Whyte's analysis of "racketeering in Cornerville" was developed along the same lines: The rackets seemed to meet a need in the community and were not looked down on there, gambling on a small scale was a widely approved form of behavior, and the structure of the gambling rackets mirrored that of respectable business in many respects.[58]

Reference to the rackets suggests more generally the matter of economic functions of deviance, which has received a great deal of attention from sociologists and other analysts. As Merton has properly remarked, morals aside, we must recognize the similarity between legitimate and illegitimate business. Both can be viewed as "industrial and professional enterprises, dispensing goods and services which some people want, for which there is a market in which goods and services are transformed into commodities. . . ." It follows, therefore, "that, in strictly economic terms, there is no relevant difference between the provision of licit and of illicit goods and services."[59] Karl Marx himself noted, in some relatively obscure writings, the relation between crime and the capitalist economic system. He pointed out that the criminal "produces" not only crime but also the entire apparatus of the police and criminal justice, as well as the professor who lectures on criminal law and later sells such lectures (in textbook form) as a market commodity. Furthermore:

Crime takes off the labour market a portion of the excess population, diminishes competition among workers, and to a certain

---

56 Merton, "Manifest and Latent Functions," in Merton, *Social Theory and Social Structure* (rev. ed.; New York: Free Press, 1959), p. 73.

57 Bell, *op. cit.*

58 William F. Whyte, *Street Corner Society* (Chicago: University of Chicago Press, 1943), pp. 111–146.

59 Merton, "Manifest and Latent Functions," p. 79.

extent stops wages from falling below the minimum, while the war against crime absorbs another part of the same population. The criminal therefore appears as one of those natural "equilibrating forces" which establish a just balance and open up a whole perspective of "useful" occupations.[60]

Similarly, an early criminological essay questioned the conventional wisdom that crime exacts a great economic toll. Arguing that many criminal offenders are in fact economically productive, E. R. Hawkins and Willard Waller insisted that professional crime not only provides many people with direct employment but also offers indirect economic benefits to many more (including manufacturers and sellers of weapons and burglary tools, the police, landlords who rent houses of prostitution and offices of detective agencies, and so on).

> More remotely, the most diverse and respectable industries are involved through our delicate interlocking exchange mechanisms. The automobile manufacturer, for example, need draw no distinction between cars that are wrecked by criminals, through carelessness or intent, or "stripped" for the parts, and those that wear out in the normal duties of producing utilities for law-abiding citizens. Wastes involved in crime are as useful from the producer's point of view as legitimate consumption. . . . If it were somehow possible to eliminate all crime suddenly, the effect on our entire economic structure would be as disastrous as the collapse of any other industry of similar magnitude. The repercussion would be the same in kind, if not degree, as that which typically follows a great war.[61]

More recently discussions of borderline crimes ("crimes without victims," involving transactions between willing buyers and sellers) have emphasized the economic underpinnings of at least one kind of deviance situation. Herbert Packer has commented:

---

[60] T. B. Bottomore and M. Rubel, eds., *Karl Marx: Selected Writings in Sociology and Social Philosophy* (London: Watts, 1956), pp. 158–159.

[61] E. R. Hawkins and Willard Waller, "Critical Notes on the Cost of Crime," *Journal of Criminal Law and Criminology*, 26 (January–February 1936), 693; see also Alfred Lindesmith, "Organized Crime," *The Annals of the American Academy of Political and Social Science*, 217 (September 1941), 119–127.

Regardless of what we think we are trying to do, when we make it illegal to traffic in commodities for which there is an inelastic demand, the effect is to secure a kind of monopoly profit to the entrepreneur who is willing to break the law. In effect we say to him: "We will set up a barrier to enter into this line of commerce by making it illegal and therefore risky; if you are willing to take the risk, you will be sheltered from the competition of those who are unwilling to do so. Of course, if we catch you, you may possibly (although not necessarily) be put out of business; but meanwhile you are free to gather the fruits that grow in the business atmosphere we are providing for you."[62]

It should be clear that these statements on the "functions of deviance" also tell us something significant about societal reactions to deviance. Some analyses within the functionalist tradition have even more directly explored the social functions of such reactions. In turning to them, we note also that psychoanalytic theory has emphasized certain rewards to the individual reactor of labeling and punishing deviation. That is, social provisions for imposing punishment afford a sanctioned outlet for aggression and hostility and further allow the punisher to hold up this act of punishment as an example to his own supposedly rebellious id impulses (thus bolstering the superego).[63] Complementing such individual-oriented analyses have been efforts to explore the social sources and patterning of the tendency to punish, including theories attributing this tendency to "moral indignation" and *ressentiment*, as well as those attempting to link "authoritarianism" to "status anxiety" and similar socially organized sentiments.[64]

[62] Herbert L. Packer, *The Limits of the Criminal Sanction* (Palo Alto: Stanford University Press, 1968), p. 279; see also Thomas C. Schelling, "Economic Analysis and Organized Crime," in President's Commission on Law Enforcement and Administration of Justice, *Task Force Report: Organized Crime* (Washington, D.C.: Government Printing Office, 1967); and Edwin M. Schur, *Crimes Without Victims* (Englewood Cliffs, N.J.: Prentice-Hall, 1967).

[63] See, for example, Franz Alexander and Hugo Staub, *The Criminal, the Judge, and the Public* (rev. ed.; New York: Free Press, 1956).

[64] See Svend Ranulf, *Moral Indignation and Middle Class Psychology* (New York: Schocken 1964); Max Scheler, *Ressentiment*, trans. by Lewis Coser (New York: Free Press, 1961); and Seymour Martin Lipset, *Political Man* (Garden City, N.Y.: Doubleday Anchor, 1963), chap. 4.

In developing a more general analysis of the social functions of reacting to deviation, Kai Erikson has taken as a point of departure Durkheim's well-known comment that crime, by virtue of our reaction to it, "brings together upright consciences and concentrates them."[65] In a similar vein, Durkheim wrote that, although punishment partly represents a passionate, somewhat nonreflective reaction, it nonetheless has an important social role. Its main function is not to correct deviators or to intimidate would-be deviators; rather it is to promote and reinforce social cohesion. Punishment is "above all designed to act upon upright people," for it serves basically to "heal the wounds made upon collective sentiments. . . ."[66] Erikson has summarized the argument that the deviating act

> creates a sense of mutuality among the people of a community by supplying a focus for group feeling. Like a war, a flood, or some other emergency, deviance makes people more alert to the interests they share in common and draws attention to those values which constitute the "collective conscience" of the community. Unless the rhythm of group life is punctuated by occasional moments of deviant behavior, presumably, social organization would be impossible.[67]

Georg Simmel made a similar point about conflict: that conflict with out-groups helps to promote internal cohesion, that conflict between various units of a social system may be a balancing mechanism rather than simply a disruptive force, and that conflict helps to define group boundaries.[68] This matter of maintaining boundaries has been emphasized by Erikson:

> The deviant is a person whose activities have moved outside the margins of the group, and when the community calls him to account for that vagrancy it is making a statement about the nature

[65] Émile Durkheim, *The Division of Labor in Society*, trans. by G. Simpson (New York: Free Press, 1947), p. 102.

[66] *Ibid.*, p. 108.

[67] Kai T. Erikson, *Wayward Puritans* (New York: Wiley, 1966), p. 4.

[68] Georg Simmel, *Conflict*, trans. by Kurt H. Wolff (New York: Free Press, 1955); see also Lewis A. Coser, *The Functions of Social Conflict* (New York: Free Press, 1956).

and placement of its boundaries. It is declaring how much variability and diversity can be tolerated within the group before it begins to lose its distinctive shape, its unique identity. [69]

Erikson has pointed out further that confrontations between deviators and reactors have always attracted much public attention and has suggested that the reason is not only the psychological appeal of such confrontations. Linking publicity and public concern about deviation to the public hangings of earlier times, he has claimed that they

> constitute one of our main sources of information about the normative outlines of society. In a figurative sense, at least, morality and immorality meet at the public scaffold, and it is during this meeting that the line between them is drawn.[70]

Through deviation, then, we construct the social meaning of conformity and delineate the boundaries of the social system. The implication that deviation cannot be eliminated is quite clear. According to Erikson, prevalent forms of deviation will vary in time and place, reflecting variations in sociocultural context. Societies will invariably, for example, display high rates of those patterns of deviation about which its members are most "concerned." Overall deviance rates will also reflect both the size and complexity of official social-control operations (and the vigor with which control agents do their work) and a particular society's sense of how much deviation is "normal" (vigorous enforcement will be directed only against those acts that exceed this limit). This reasoning suggests a final point, made by Erikson and other recent analysts: that our social arrangements may actually be organized to maintain, if not to promote, deviating behavior. This result is particularly apparent in situations involving patently unenforceable criminal laws and other "patterned evasions" of norms; because of conflicting values related to the activities in

---

[69] Erikson, *op. cit.*, p. 11; see also George Herbert Mead, "The Psychology of Punitive Justice," *American Journal of Sociology*, 23 (1928), 557–602; and Coser, "Some Functions of Deviant Behavior and Normative Flexibility," *American Journal of Sociology*, 68 (September 1962), 171–181.

[70] Erikson, *op. cit.*, p. 12.

question, the relevant legal and other social-control measures are more accurately described as efforts at "regulation" than as attempts at eliminating the offending behavior.[71]

These comments should suggest the very close ties that exist between the functionalist and labeling approaches to deviance. It is not fortuitous that an analysis like that of Erikson, which clearly draws on functional perspectives, simultaneously exhibits the hallmarks of a labeling approach. Quite simply, those writers who have explored the social functions of deviance—either generally or in connection with particular forms of deviation—have also developed significant ideas on the *societal reaction* to deviance. The functions of deviance and the functions of reactions to deviance are two sides of the same coin. Studies of the former indicate how deeply particular deviations are rooted in a sociocultural context; investigations of the latter reveal that society's reactions to such deviations are shaped precisely by these deep roots. Although functionalist theory itself may thus provide no framework for intensive analysis of the specific *processes* involved in societal reactions to deviating behavior, it does help us to specify some of the broad factors affecting such reactions, particularly in collective rule-making. In this respect, it is quite consistent with, and in fact complements, the major findings of labeling-oriented research.

Conflict, labeling, and resistance to labeling[72]

We have already observed that an analysis of aspects of social conflict must be included in any labeling approach to deviance and control. At each of the three levels of analysis mentioned earlier, elements of conflict are

71 See Robin Williams, *American Society: A Sociological Interpretation* (2nd ed.; New York: Knopf, 1960), chap. 10; see also Schur, *op. cit.*

72 We are grateful to Alan M. Orenstein for his many perceptive comments regarding issues considered in this section.

inherent in the social reactions to deviation and in efforts at social control. At each level and for any particular kind of deviation or potential deviation, what Lofland has called "conflict games" are present. Opposing "forces"—be they pressure groups or subcultures at the collective decision-making level, actors and others on the interpersonal level, or "clients" and control agencies at the organizational-processing level—struggle to define situations, types of behavior, specific acts, and the essential "character" of particular individuals. Through these conflict processes emerge the various "outcomes" that we noted earlier. Some types of behavior come to be defined as conformist, some as deviant. Through interaction with significant others some individuals learn to see themselves as "normal," whereas others begin to see themselves as abnormal or as wrongdoers. Still other individuals come to be publicly and officially defined as deviators, perhaps even as "criminals," whereas some to whom formal labeling processes are initially applied eventually are exonerated of the "charges" leveled against them.

In considering factors affecting the development of deviant identity, Lofland has remarked, "other things being equal, the greater the *consistency, duration* and *intensity* with which a definition is promoted by Others about an Actor, the greater the likelihood that an Actor will embrace that definition as truly applicable to himself."[73] Unfortunately, this statement (though perhaps basically sound) does not take us very far, for we must recognize one or the other of two important qualifications: First, we know full well that "all other things" are rarely if ever equal; second, the factors that influence the consistency, duration, and intensity with which a definition is imposed vary, depending upon the situation. Although we can make some kinds of broad generalizations about probable deviance outcomes, they are thus uncertain guides to prediction of specific types of deviation or particular categories of individuals.

For example, Table 3 shows the general relation between *resources* (for the moment unspecified) and *outcomes* at the vari-

[73] Lofland, *op. cit.,* p. 122.

Table 3 Relation between salient resources and deviance outcomes

	INTERPERSONAL REACTIONS	ORGANIZATIONAL PROCESSING	COLLECTIVE RULE-MAKING
High resources (of individual or group)	High ability to resist imputations of deviant identity or to "manage" desired deviant roles successfully	High resistance to processing efforts Low rates of "official" deviance	Dominant social perception of individual or group norms as "conformist" High ability to impose rules
Low resources (of individual or group)	Low ability to resist imputations of deviant identity or to manage desired deviant roles successfully	Low resistance to processing efforts High rates of "official" deviance	Dominant social perception of individual or group norms as "deviant" Low ability to impose rules

ous levels of analysis. Clearly groups and individuals with high resources are more likely than are those with low resources to be able to avoid or resist negative labeling. But the crucial question remains: What are the relevant resources? The answer is not obvious. We immediately think, of course, of "standard" sociological variables that might influence these outcomes: socioeconomic status, age, sex, education, and so on. Indeed, we have already noted Becker's comment that by and large the poor, racial minorities, women, and the young in our society tend to have rules imposed on them by the more powerful segments of the population. Similarly, Lofland has suggested that "When low education and youth or old age are combined in the same Actor . . . it seems apparent that he becomes especially vulnerable to escalation [to deviant identity]."[74] But there are several problems in using such standard variables to analyze specific deviance situations. The first is that the salience of a particular variable in determining the probability of deviating acts or the susceptibility to labeling varies with the type of deviation being considered. A youth may thus appear to have a relatively high probability of "vagrancy" and high susceptibility to labeling as "vagrant" yet a relatively low probability of committing forgery and of being labeled a forger (or a tax evader or an embezzler). Although this example suggests the effect of a combination of personal status characteristics and "opportunity," not all variations in susceptibility are attributable to such combinations. For example, the probability that blacks will engage in armed robbery (and be labeled "robbers") is relatively high, yet for homosexual behavior the probability is approximately the same as that for whites. Presumably, opportunity is not a key factor in this variability. On the contrary, it seems that race has little or no importance in determining either probability of homosexual activity or susceptibility and resistance to labeling as homosexual. Other factors, including perhaps the strength of masculine self-concepts, particular family-background and early socialization factors, and the like, may be more salient in this kind of deviation.

[74] *Ibid.*, p. 181.

A second major complication is that the effects of a given variable may not always work in the same *direction* in determining the probability of engaging in a particular deviation, on one hand, and susceptibility to labeling as that kind of deviator, on the other. The variable of race appears to operate in the same direction in both aspects for the deviation of armed robbery, whereas for drug addiction the occupational status of a doctor seems to operate in different directions. When other things are equal, doctors have a higher probability of becoming addicts than do others, yet they also have greater resistance to (higher probability of avoiding) being labeled addicts, at least officially. One explanation may lie in doctors' greater "opportunity," that is, their easy access to drugs. Opportunity, rather than high occupational status, is thus the salient variable. These observations, in turn, suggest a possible generalization: Status characteristics of the individual tend to operate in one direction in determining the probability of a specific deviation and the susceptibility to negative labeling, whereas opportunity factors tend to operate in opposite directions in determining the two aspects.

This difference seems to result from conditions in which opportunity is a salient factor in determining initial deviation, conditions that imply a certain amount of protection, or insulation, for the deviator. As the doctor has both access to drugs and insulation from detection (*because of* his legitimate access to drugs), so the bank teller has both opportunity to embezzle and some protection against discovery; the youth immersed in a delinquent subculture is to some extent shielded by his membership even as it affords him special opportunities for deviating. In a sense, then, a certain amount of resistance to negative labeling is built into what we call "opportunity."

When we turn to a third major category of variables traditionally used to "explain" the deviating acts of individuals—social-psychological factors like individual alienation, weak masculine self-concepts, various personality traits attributed to particular family situations, and so on—we find that they too seem to operate in one direction in determining the likelihood of initial deviating acts and the susceptibility to negative labeling. For example, the strength or stability of sexual identity seems to be a highly salient characteristic in determining homosexual behavior. Presumably males with strong masculine self-concepts are less likely to engage in homosexual activities and are also relatively unsusceptible or resistant to labeling as "homosexual." The same unity of direction seems typical of other social-psychological variables as well. The individual whose psychological problems or personality state increases the probability of his engaging in some form of deviation probably has, at the same time and because of this condition, weaker resistance to any labeling efforts directed against him than does the person with greater psychological "stability."

Of course, additional problems intrude between these broad generalizations about relative probabilities and more specific efforts at prediction. For purposes of analysis we have treated these variables as if they acted separately and as if for each particular kind of deviation only one were salient. Yet we can assume that this simplicity is not accurate. Just as individuals display various constellations of possibly relevant characteristics in the three categories, so may some combinations be salient for the generation of particular kinds of deviating behavior (and the susceptibility to particular kinds of negative labeling). Furthermore, we must remember that an individual's or a group's resources for resisting labeling processes do not remain constant. On the contrary, such resources tend to be affected by those very same processes. Although the strength of an individual's sexual identity may partly determine his resistance to labeling as a sexual deviant, active efforts to define him thus (even efforts that are not totally "successful") may, in turn, affect his sexual identity. At the level of collective decision-making, the pressure groups or segments with greatest power tend to impose the rules, but any "political" setbacks that such groups experience will in turn reduce their power (and thus indirectly diminish their ability to impose rules or to resist the rules that others would impose upon them).

Finally, an absolutely central consideration for the labeling orientation is that the generalizations presented here cannot adequately account for the diverse processing contingencies arising at the different levels and operating at least somewhat independently of the predictor variables in question. These statements of relative probability do, it is true, partly incorporate what we know about some of these contingent processes. That is, built into our statement that blacks have relatively low resistance to negative labeling of some sort is our knowledge of differing responses of individuals and control agencies to the behavior of blacks and whites. The existence of additional and contingent factors (like organizational imperatives), that shape response processes and do not depend solely upon the characteristics of the individuals responded to makes it very difficult however, to relate the predictor variables to final deviance "outcomes" analytically.

Labeling and
predictive theory

If we keep these points in mind, together with the important fact that deviating acts and deviant roles are sometimes sought by individuals, rather than thrust upon them, then we can easily understand why efforts to relate quantitatively grounded and prediction-oriented theories to labeling analysis run into serious difficulties. Figure 1 depicts a framework for beginning such an attempt. If we view traditional theories of deviance as explanations of different rates of entry into institutionalized labeling processes, then we have some basis for considering these theories and the labeling approach as concerned with different parts of a unified scheme of action.

From the point of view of prediction-oriented theories, however, the "deviance" resulting from this scheme of action would be the "rates" (presumably the official rates) of individual deviation. If we knew rate differentials for "actual" deviation (as approximated, for example, in the findings from "self-reported behavior" studies), as well as the rate differentials in the official statistics, we might then claim that the difference between the

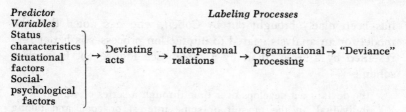

Figure 1   An attempt to relate predictor variables and labeling processes

two represents the impact of "labeling." For example, if official statistics showed armed robberies by blacks and whites to be in a ratio of 10/2 yet data on the actual commission of such acts revealed only a 3/2 ratio, the outcome could be viewed as having been partly "produced" by or through the intervening labeling processes. Such an interpretation may hold up as a partial "explanation" of official rates, though even on this level it is of limited value, for it does not really tell us how this "production" occurs. But such an attempt to "compute" the role of labeling is more seriously deficient on another ground: It treats the individual's behavior, as reflected in rates, as the only "outcome" requiring explanation.

As we have seen, a broadly based labeling approach is concerned with several levels of analysis and with several kinds of deviance "outcomes." Even in its attention to the individual deviator, labeling analysis focuses on matters that cannot easily be quantified in this way: the development of deviant self-concepts and the elaboration of deviant "roles" and "careers." As the traditional and labeling approaches basically seek to "explain" different "results" (even as regards the deviating individual), we cannot expect to link them in a quantitatively unified (and at the same time theoretically coherent), analytic model. Furthermore, the probabilistic, prediction-oriented conception of causation common to traditional analyses is not well suited to the labeling analyst's exploration of deviance outcomes. Again, even in connection with the deviating behavior of individuals, the emphasis of the labeling approach on both processing contingencies and actor choice render quantifiable predictions inappropriate. This point has been nicely brought out by Cohen, who has noted that the model for an analysis geared to interaction processes is better represented by a "tree" than by a table (see Figure 2). In such a scheme

> the deviant act develops over time through a series of stages. Some individual, in the pursuit of some interest or goal, and taking account of the situation, makes a move, possibly in a deviant direction, possibly with no thought of deviance in mind. However, his next move—the continuation of his course of action—is not fully determined by the state of affairs at the beginning. He may, at this juncture, choose among two or more possible directions. Which it will be will depend on the state of the actor and situation at *this* point in time, and either or both may, in the meantime, have undergone change. . . . The completed pathway A, AA, AAA— here represented by solid lines—is the course of action that, according to the theory, culminates in deviance. The other pathways, represented by broken lines, are the other courses that action *could* have taken. Pathways are not predictable from initial states or initial acts alone; prediction is *contingent* on the state of affairs following each move.[75]

Although such a scheme does suggest how contingencies (including the crucial responses of others) affect the individual's course of action, it is incomplete from a labeling point of view if the culmination of the interaction process is viewed simply in terms of deviating behavior. We may recall a point stressed earlier: that adherents of the labeling orientation are really less interested in the *causes* of individual deviation than in the *consequences* for the individual, and for the social system more generally, of his acting in a way that is treated as deviant. Provided that we consider "deviant identity" and "deviant careers" as among the outcomes of the interaction process, the "tree" diagram holds up well for analysis of the individual deviator. Just such a contingent, shifting course of action is involved in the development of deviant self-concepts and commitment to deviant roles, as well as in the production of deviating acts.

It must be reiterated, however, that the scope of the labeling

---

[75] Cohen, *Deviance and Control* (Englewood Cliffs, N.J.: Prentice-Hall, 1966), pp. 44, 45.

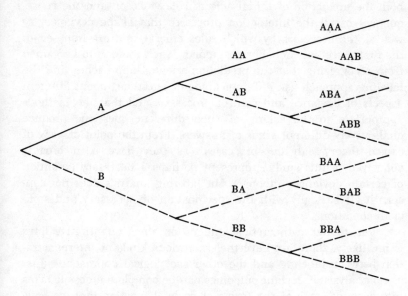

Figure 2   Interaction process and deviant outcomes
SOURCE: Albert K. Cohen, *Deviance and Control* (Englewood Cliffs, N.J.:
Prentice-Hall, 1966), p. 43.

approach extends well beyond the individual deviator. For example, the various research questions posed in our earlier discussion
of collective decision-making (in which we recognized the processes of rule-making at the societal level as a kind of, or part of, a
"labeling process") simply cannot be addressed in terms of the
"tree" scheme just presented. Similarly, the "tree" scheme cannot
do justice either to the role of organizational imperatives (although organizational reactions are indeed among the contingencies considered to shape the individual's course of action) or to
those secondary ramifications of deviance situations (like illegal
"markets") the effects of which are broad and diffuse, going beyond impact upon individual deviators.

It should be clear from this discussion that the attempt to
"quantify" a labeling analysis—in the sense of including it in
some broader, quantitative analytic model that would include

both the prediction of initial acts of rule violation and the consequences of all the interaction processes that shape deviance, as well as the processes by which rules emerge and are imposed in the first place—is probably misguided. Much more is to be gained from recognizing that the prediction-oriented approaches and the labeling approach ask different kinds of questions, about different aspects of deviance and control processes, and that the methods appropriate to the asking of such different questions produce qualitatively different *kinds* of answers. From the point of view of causal theory, labeling processes (as they have been broadly conceived in this study) represent perhaps a necessary condition of certain deviance outcomes, but labeling analysis does not concern itself basically with the specification of necessary and sufficient conditions.

Yet, though a theoretical integration along quantitative lines is not likely, there are nevertheless various kinds of interpenetration between labeling and the other sociological approaches. Just as no analysis of deviant outcomes can be complete unless it takes into account some of the forms of societal reaction that we have considered here, so the analysis of labeling processes invariably involves applications of "functional theory," "conflict theory," and other standard modes of sociological conceptualization. Similarly, there is a reciprocal relation between the operation of what we have called "predictor variables" and societal reaction processes. As Cohen has noted, opportunity structures may determine initial deviation, but social reactions to such deviation will significantly determine future opportunities.[76]

We reiterate that a labeling approach is in fact solidly grounded in conventional sociological theory, not only in the symbolic interactionism upon which it draws most directly, but also in other theoretical traditions whose contributions to it are more indirect. The necessary conclusion, it seems, is that, though in its broadest meaning labeling is essential to comprehensive analysis of deviance situations, it cannot by itself provide answers to all the relevant questions. But any such attempt by one of the allegedly "opposing" theories is by itself equally doomed to failure.

[76] Cohen, "The Sociology of the Deviant Act," pp. 10–12.

WHAT, if any, are the distinctive moral and policy implications of the labeling approach? It is interesting that the orientation has received quite contradictory interpretations in this regard; indeed, it is even tempting to suggest that the meaning of labeling analysis itself lies "in the eye of the beholder." Some commentators consider the approach as reflecting a kind of social radicalism that calls into question conventional definitions and institutions; others claim that its concentration on individual social psychology and small-scale interactions renders it nearly apolitical (if not, by indirection, politically conservative). Some critics charge labeling analysts with romantic sentimentalizing of wrongdoers and unwillingness to recognize the responsibility of such individuals for their own behavior. On the other hand and somewhat paradoxically, labeling analysts themselves sometimes view the approach as a vehicle for denying older "determinisms" and a basis for reasserting the values of personal freedom and individual responsibility.

In this apparent confusion one point seems certain: Whatever its more specific implications, the labeling approach does highlight the value-laden nature of deviance and control problems. As we have seen, both the growing attention of American sociologists to this general topic and the development or revival of the orientations considered in this book are partly attributable to discontent with the apparent results of adopting a natural-science model for social research, of attempting to confront problems of deviation from a narrowly quantitative, "value free" perspective. The labeling approach makes clear in a number of ways that some consideration of values is essential to an analysis of deviance. The central theme, that men "create" deviance by defining certain forms of behavior and certain individuals as such, amounts to a radical restatement of Willard Waller's earlier insistence that social "problems" occur only through the making of value judgments. As we have also noted, the labeling approach highlights the significance of conflict elements in these definitional processes, thus showing the basically "political" nature of deviance. The labeling analyst's recognition that, from the deviator's point of view, the conformist may be considered the "outsider," or "deviant," emphasizes still further the crucial role of values in this area.

Beyond this general point, however, the moral and policy implications of labeling analysis are not as clear as either its proponents or its critics may claim. This confusion is the result partly of theoretical ambiguities inherent in the labeling perspective and partly of the simple reemphasis on certain central tenets of sociological and social-psychological theory. Analysis of social situations in terms of such tenets does not necessarily carry "radical" or "conservative" implications; on the contrary, the inferences drawn from such analysis may well vary according to the policy or "political" preferences of the particular interpreter. Although recognition that men create situations through processes of social definition informs us that such situations may be neither "natural" nor "inevitable," it does not provide answers to the persistent question of which substantive definitions are "desirable," "moral," or "right" and "should be" applied to particular situations. The problem is similar to that which confronts the functional theorist. A specification of the "functions" or "dysfunctions" of a given social arrangement may tell us something about its prospects for stability or susceptibility to change, yet it cannot by itself provide a moral or policy-oriented evaluation of the various possible "functional alternatives."

One of the central ambiguities of the labeling perspective has already been mentioned, that arising from the underlying conception of the nature of social action. On one hand, by shifting attention from the actor himself to the social reactions that his behavior elicits, the labeling approach seems to suggest that he has relatively little "to do with" his deviance; he simply "suffers from contingencies" in that his particular behavior patterns have summoned forth negative responses. It may seem that we are being asked to view the deviant primarily as having been "put upon" by others or as "a passive nonentity who is responsible neither for his suffering nor its alleviation—who is more 'sinned against than sinning.' "[1] On the other hand, analysts of the labeling and related schools react strongly against formulations designed to "explain" human behavior in terms of the constraining impact on the individual of external "determinants"; in particular they see neither psychological nor social "pathology" as an adequate explanatory conception.

There is, as we have seen, an important theme of voluntarism in both symbolic interactionism and the phenomenological-existential tradition, in which the individual, far from being viewed as a passive object who is pushed this way and that by external forces, is considered actively to respond to those around him, to reflect upon himself and his impression on others, to project his desired courses of action, and thus to participate positively in the shaping of his own "destiny." As Peter Berger has expressed it:

> It is quite correct to say that society is objective fact, coercing and even creating us. But it is also correct to say that our own meaningful acts help to support the edifice of society and may on

[1] Alvin W. Gouldner, "The Sociologist as Partisan: Sociology and the Welfare State," *The American Sociologist,* 3 (May 1968), 106; see also Judith Lorber, "Deviance as Performance: The Case of Illness," *Social Problems,* 14 (Winter 1967), 302–310.

occasion help to change it. Indeed, the two statements contain between them the paradox of social existence: That society defines
us, but is in turn defined by us. . . . We need the recognition of
society to be human, to have an image of ourselves, to have an
identity. But society needs the recognition of many like us in order
to exist at all . . . the control systems are in constant need of
confirmation and re-confirmation by those they are meant to
control. It is possible to withhold such confirmation in a number
of ways. . . .[2]

In stressing that deviance outcomes emerge from the continuous *inter*action between the individual's behavior and the responses of others, labeling analysts, far from treating individuals
as passive objects, appear to challenge the tendency of other
theorists to treat them as such and do in fact recognize significant
measures of "freedom" and "personal dignity."

The moral and policy questions involve the extent to which
personal "responsibility" for his behavior ought be imputed to the
deviator. How far we wish to go in that direction depends, in turn,
partly upon the kind of balance we believe exists between the
individual's freedom of action and the ability of reactors to control
his situation. Some labeling-oriented or symbolic-interactionist
writers seem to attribute considerable freedom of action to the
deviator, even though they also usually seek to avoid entanglement
in the conventional controversy over freedom and determinism.
In reaction to what David Matza has characterized as the "hard
determinism" underlying early criminological studies,[3] some analysts of deviance have thus adopted a rather extreme version of
what might be called "hard antideterminism." For example, in
recent writings by Frank Hartung on criminality and by Thomas
Szasz on mental illness,[4] we find strong declarations of rational
bases for deviations that previously had been viewed from a de-

[2] Peter L. Berger, *Invitation to Sociology* (Garden City, N.Y.: Doubleday
Anchor, 1963), pp. 128–129.
[3] David Matza, *Delinquency and Drift* (New York: Wiley, 1964).
[4] Frank Hartung, *Crime, Law and Society* (Detroit: Wayne State University
Press, 1965); and Thomas S. Szasz, *The Myth of Mental Illness* (New York:
Hoeber, 1961).

terministic vantage point, as well as considerable willingness to impute to actors "responsibility" for their behavior. Szasz has argued in support of his belief that mental illness is a "myth," that people who are troublesome because of various "problems of living" should not be subjected to involuntary psychiatric "treatment" or commitment. Unless they themselves seek psychiatric help voluntarily, they should be either left alone or (if their actions create real danger to others) be held accountable and punished under the criminal law.[5]

Other labeling analysts apparently seek a middle path between viewing deviators as either "sick" or "bad" and considering them as "simply different" (Szasz also makes this effort, but with perhaps limited success); they speak of "residual deviance" and of processes in which the individual "drifts" into deviance.[6] Yet Matza, in describing the latter processes, has spelled out how delinquency may be activated among youths in such a state of "drift" and has defined the role of "will" in such a way that his analysis veers toward "hard antideterminism." Will, he has declared, "is something that may or may not be excercised. Will is an option."[7]

Matza's attribution of freedom of action to the deviator has become even more pronounced in his recent *Becoming Deviant*.[8] In reanalyzing Howard Becker's study of marihuana use, Matza presents his own central theme at the outset: ". . . the process will be rendered *easy* and open; it becomes apparent that *anyone* can become a marihuana user and that *no one* has to." Continuing in this vein, he returns to the notion of "option" from his earlier work. Exposure to the opportunity to use marihuana does not force one into deviant activity; rather, one experiences only the option

---

5 Szasz, *Law, Liberty and Psychiatry* (New York: Macmillan, 1963); and Szasz, *Psychiatric Justice* (New York: Macmillan, 1965); see also Edwin M. Schur, "Psychiatrists Under Attack: The Rebellious Dr. Szasz," *The Atlantic* (June 1966), 72–76.

6 Thomas J. Scheff, *Being Mentally Ill* (Chicago: Aldine, 1966); and Matza, *op. cit.*

7 *Ibid.*, p. 191.

8 Matza, *Becoming Deviant* (Englewood Cliffs, N.J.: Prentice-Hall, 1969), especially chap. 6.

to use it or not. Both the beginning of deviant activity and its continuation depend upon the individual himself.

> By being willing, the subject may begin a process that neither holds him within its grip nor unfolds without him. Without the subject, the process has no meaning since it must be mediated through him and take its form from him. To enter the process, the invitational edge of the deviant phenomenon must somehow be hurdled. To do that a leap is required—an act of will; the phenomenon is engaged, but not abstractly. The subject is actually doing the thing—an immersion in concrete activity which is essential. The remainder of the process of becoming deviant can hardly happen if the subject continues to gaze at a phenomenon kept at a distance.[9]

Matza has described the individual's participation in even more active terms, claiming that at certain stages in the process of becoming deviant the subject "makes up his mind, literally." Although he has recognized that the individual "does sometimes have empty authority, a subjectivity oppressed by context or circumstance," he has undercut this recognition with the claim that peer influence is "a matter to be considered by the subject. . . ."[10] Although it is, of course, true that the individual reflects to some extent upon the circumstances and individuals affecting his behavior, the implication that he can decide how much influence they will have seems rather extreme. Matza has provided no real evidence that the process that he has described actually occurs, either invariably or even frequently, and he has certainly adduced no data in support of its primacy. Furthermore, the example of marihuana use seems a loaded one, for this type of deviation is one in which fairly free choice is known to be frequently if not typically a significant factor. It is not at all clear that Matza's interpretation would be valid if applied to other types of deviation.

At least in the absence of hard data, such an interpretation remains largely academic. What may be more to the point is the fact that varying notions about freedom of action and personal

9 *Ibid.*, p. 117.
10 *Ibid.*, pp. 122, 124.

responsibility for behavior are held by individuals who deviate and by individuals who respond to deviation. Efforts have been made to determine empirically what such notions are, and there is thus at least a partial basis for assessing their significance.[11] At least two different patterns of individual deviators' views on responsibility for their acts seem to exist. On one hand, as we have seen, there is sometimes a running struggle between those reactors who view a type of deviation as evidence of sickness or maladjustment and the deviators themselves, who seek to define their behavior as simply different from that currently dominant. The implication seems to be that such deviators consider themselves "responsible" for their actions, which they view as morally acceptable. On the other hand, there are times when deviating individuals or groups seek to project images of their behavior as "beyond their control," either applying a "medical model" to their actions or conditions or stressing the impact of other external "determinants." For example, a recent study of Alcoholics Anonymous has noted the extent to which that organization has employed an "illness" interpretation of alcoholism to elicit relatively favorable public response.[12] At any rate, it does often seem that deviators are alert to the possible "responsibility implications" of their behavior and that they may engage in "performance" designed to project certain images of themselves in this regard. As Judith Lorber has commented, "the deviant often more or less deliberately conveys an impression which he hopes will lead to the imposition of a certain label by his audience."[13]

As for the views of reactors to deviation, Stoll has cited various research findings showing that individuals and agencies that hold deterministic views tend to be less punitive in their reactions than are those that adopt voluntaristic interpretations.[14] It seems

[11] See, for example, Clarice S. Stoll, "Images of Man and Social Control," *Social Forces,* 47 (December 1968), 119–127.

[12] Harrison M. Trice and Paul M. Roman, "Delabeling, Relabeling, and Alcoholics Anonymous," *Social Problems,* 17 (Spring 1970), 538–546.

[13] Lorber, *op. cit.,* p. 309; see also Vilhelm Aubert and Sheldon Messinger, "The Criminal and the Sick," *Inquiry,* 3 (1958), 137–160.

[14] Stoll, *op. cit.*

clear that the reactors' assumptions about freedom and responsibility will affect policies toward deviation and, at least indirectly, individual deviant "careers" as well. Perhaps the clearest example has been the underlying philosophy of the juvenile-court movement and its impact on the processing of delinquents. As we have noted, the application of a "rehabilitative ideal" (itself based heavily on deterministic assumptions about the initiation of delinquency) has been a substantial factor affecting the processing and labeling of delinquents. This example also suggests that academic theories about freedom and responsibility can have an impact in the real world, to the extent that they come to be translated into the ideologies and everyday practices of social-control organizations. It should, however, also be noted that, as Stoll has reminded us, control agents do not always share a clear-cut ideological consensus on a particular form of deviation.

> It seems likely that consensus within an occupation [a category or organization of control agents] would be least for those types of deviance at the margins of the so-called pure types (crime, sin, illness, disloyalty). Included in the marginal types of deviance are mental illness, addictive diseases, sexual abnormalities.

Lack of consensus has an impact on deviating individuals: Contradictions in the ideologies of deviance held by various agents will create "strains in the social control network" and will tend to "place the deviant in role strain."[15]

Some observers have specified the matter of responsibility as a central element in the sociological definition of deviance. Jack Douglas, for example, has declared that "the fundamental problem is that of determining the conditions of responsibility: under what conditions is an individual considered by members of our society to be (morally) responsible for a given event?"[16] Similarly, Peter McHugh has argued that "a deviant act is an act that members deem 'might not have been,' or 'might have been otherwise';

---

15 *Ibid.*, pp. 122. 124,

16 Jack D. Douglas, "Deviance and Respectability: The Social Construction of Moral Meanings," in Douglas, ed., *Deviance and Respectability* (New York: Basic Books, 1970), p. 12.

second, it is an act the agent of which is deemed to 'know what he's doing.' "[17] It is certainly true that, as Eliot Freidson has suggested, imputation of responsibility is a "critical dimension" in defining and reacting to deviations: "It seems to be critical in that it bears closely on the moral identity of the person concerned and on the obligations others may feel toward him."[18] To build the element of personal responsibility directly into the definition of deviance itself would, however, as our earlier discussion suggested, result in too narrow a definition. As we have seen, there are conditions like blindness for which the individuals involved are not held morally "responsible"; yet the reactions to such conditions warrant their inclusion in the category of deviance. Freidson has made this point well:

> . . . the simple moral dichotomy of responsibility does not allow for the halo of moral evaluation that in fact surrounds many types of behavior for which, theoretically, people are not held responsible, but which in some way damage their identities. Some diseases, such as syphilis, leprosy, and even tuberculosis, are surrounded with loathing even though they are all "merely" infections. And many forms of organic dysfunction or maldevelopment for which the sufferer is not held responsible occasion responses of fear or disgust—epilepsy, dwarfism, and disfigurement, for example.[19]

There is good reason, therefore, to use the dimension of responsibility and nonresponsibility as a partial basis for suggesting types of deviance, as Freidson has done, rather than insisting that imputation of responsibility is a necessary condition of any deviance at all.

Interwined with these issues of freedom and responsibility and most relevant in assessing moral and policy implications of the labeling approach are questions arising from the relativistic emphasis and the sympathetic research stance adopted by the

[17] Peter McHugh, "A Common-Sense Conception of Deviance," in Douglas, ed., *Deviance and Respectability* (New York: Basic Books, 1970), p. 61.
[18] Eliot Freidson, "Disability as Social Deviance," in Marvin B. Sussman, ed., *Sociology and Rehabilitation* (Washington, D.C.: American Sociological Association, 1965), p. 76.
[19] *Ibid.*, p. 79.

labeling analyst. What are the implications of the fact that the labeling school and related orientations seem to represent a kind of "underdog" sociology? As we saw earlier, central to this body of work are a thoroughgoing willingness to view deviations in a non-evaluative way and at the same time a strong disposition toward analyzing deviance situations as they appear to the individuals directly experiencing them (perhaps particularly those "labeled" deviant). In "Whose Side Are We On?"[20] Becker has commented that, in seeming to "side" with the deviator (by viewing the situation from his point of view), the labeling analyst has actually simply refused to acknowledge and defer to the conventional "hierarchy of credibility." It is part of the established status order that the rule-makers and rule-enforcers have the "right" to define deviance situations; to explore alternative definitions of these situations seems biased (sometimes even to the researchers themselves) precisely because acceptance of this established moral hierarchy is so deeply ingrained.

In line with this interpretation, Becker has noted further that the tendency to charge the researcher with bias is most often apparent and least effectively resisted in connection with deviance situations that have remained fairly "apolitical." When a type of deviation is widely acknowledged as reflecting "political" or social conflict, analyzing it from other than the dominant point of view appears more acceptable because the conventional credibility hierarchy has already been called into question by others and not just by sociologists. As Becker has insisted, deviance situations always involve superordinates and subordinates (recall our earlier stress on the inevitable power elements in such situations). Furthermore, there is no avoiding the fact that in analyzing such situations we inevitably see them from "someone's point of view" or at least in a way that coincides with someone's point of view. The best that we can do is to be explicit about the point of view and the limits of our research perspective, in order to avoid sentimentality and,

20 Howard S. Becker, "Whose Side Are We On?" *Social Problems,* 14 (Winter 1967), 239–247.

as far as possible, to employ all available methodological and common-sense safeguards against distortion.

Although its challenge to the credibility hierarchy seems to suggest that labeling analysis is somewhat "radical" in its political leanings, Alvin Gouldner has argued that, on the contrary, its research focus implies a rather conservative perspective on the problems of modern society.[21] Admitting that a "sociology of the underdog" is justified because deviants undergo much suffering that is both unnecessary and largely hidden from public view, Gouldner has nonetheless considered the labeling approach (in particular the work of Becker) as romanticizing certain nonpolitical deviations and avoiding a truly radical critique of the social system as a whole. Labeling analysis, he has claimed, focuses unduly upon the activities of local officials, while avoiding direct scrutiny or analysis of the national establishment. Even if this accusation were justified, Gouldner's interpretation of the reasons for this focus is not very convincing. Declaring that the new perspectives on deviance may afford an easy avenue to professional attention for young sociologists and that "sociologists with liberal ideologies will more likely adopt underdog perspectives when they experience these as compatible with the pursuit of their own career interests," Gouldner has related these perspectives to the alleged concentration on local officialdom: ". . . the respectables who are being resisted, and whose hierarchy of credibility is disputed, are those local officials who, for most part, do not control access to large supplies of research funds." According to Gouldner, the new underdog sociology is "the sociology of young men with friends in Washington."[22]

It is true that the new approaches to deviance, especially the ethnomethodological orientation, have sometimes been in danger of developing faddish or cultish qualities. Yet to attribute involvement in such research and analysis solely or even largely to potential career "payoffs" seems unwarranted. The same argument could, of course, be made about any orientation or body of work

21 Gouldner, *op. cit.*
22 *Ibid.*, pp. 108, 110.

that has a substantial amount of professional standing, an observation that serves only to confirm the argument's general inadequacy. In his efforts to develop a "sociology of sociology," Gouldner has seemed quite unwilling to confront the labeling approach on its own terms, to accord it respect as a serious intellectual undertaking. If he had done so, for example, he might well have perceived a perfectly sound theoretical basis for relatively high attention to the acts of local officials: They are among the most important of the direct labelers of deviants and are thus of special concern.

Actually, however, labeling analysts have not focused exclusively upon local reactors. On the contrary, their work has included analyses of national legislation and national law-enforcement agencies, as well as of broad sociopolitical movements. And, as we have seen, a broadly conceived labeling approach is strongly concerned with rule-making at the societal level, as well as with more specific enforcement of rules at the local level. Nor is it true, to this writer's knowledge, that the proponents of an "underdog" sociology of deviance are especially beholden to Federal agencies for research funding. Certainly they have not shied away from criticism of Federal laws and policies: Perhaps the best example is their continuous strong attack on Federal narcotics laws and enforcement agencies.

Gouldner's complaint seems basically to rest on the fact that he and the labeling theorists tend to be interested in studying different kinds of problems. Whereas he is primarily interested in analysis of the political, socioeconomic, and racial conflicts in American society, the labelists focus more typically (though by no means exclusively) on the areas to which we often apply the terms "crime," "vice," "sin," and "illness." Whereas the policy implications of research along the lines of Gouldner's preference may be directly related to broad issues of socioeconomic and political change, those of labeling research are more likely to be directly related to changes in the criminal law, in public attitudes toward certain kinds of behavior, and in the accepted ways of dealing with "troublesome" people and situations. Although Gouldner might presumably argue that the area of greatest interest to him is more "important" than that which most interests the labeling researchers, surely both have sociological and social significance.

On balance, then, what is our assessment of the moral and policy implications of labeling analysis? First, we reemphasize the roots of the labeling approach in certain basic formulations of classic sociological theory. Whatever changes in moral outlook and public policy may be promoted by labeling research cannot be attributed solely to its unique features. At the same time, the labeling orientation does have some distinctive emphases, and they may well exert an impact on attitudes and policies toward deviance and social control. Among such major policy effects we may cite at least five.

First, its strong relativism reinforces the growing challenge to conventional thinking about problems of deviation, a challenge that has itself, as we have seen, partly contributed to the current popularity of the labeling approach.

Second, by stressing conflict elements, and by focusing on rule-making processes, labeling analysis makes clear that problems of deviance and control are also "value" and "political" problems.

Third, through research on social-control processes and agencies, the labeling approach has attracted a great deal of public attention to deficiencies in our control apparatus.

Fourth, by dramatizing the stigmatizing nature of negative labeling, the approach has probably led to somewhat greater caution in the use of negative labels and to less glib resort to euphemistic terminology for processes that are not less harsh or punishing.

Fifth, the voluntaristic theme underlying some labeling analyses may have served a useful purpose in causing various specialists to reassess earlier, largely unquestioned deterministic assumptions about the causes of deviance.

Apart perhaps from promoting a very broad injunction to "avoid unnecessary labeling," the orientation does not seem to provide a clear-cut general direction for public policy toward deviating behavior. On the contrary, the policy impact of labeling-oriented research is probably going to vary, depending upon the type of deviance involved, the specific nature of existing control policies and practices, and the other social forces affecting the course of policy in that particular area. For example, although research on labeling processes has helped to promote changes in the juvenile-court system, such changes also have reflected new outlooks derived partly from other sources, like arguments long advanced by legal critics of the system.[23]

Overall, the labeling orientation carries the potential to generate either broad-scale and basically "political" or narrowly social-psychological and essentially "apolitical" studies—or both. Gouldner has recently captured this dual potential in a comment on Erving Goffman's work:

> On the one side, it has an implication of being *against* the existent hierarchies and hence against those advantaged by them; it is, to this extent, infused with a rebel vision critical of modern society. On the other side, however, Goffman's rejection of hierarchy often expresses itself as an *avoidance* of social stratification and of the importance of power differences, even for concerns that are central to him; thus it entails an accommodation to existent power arrangements.[24]

Which type of impact the labeling school will have will depend largely upon which version of labeling analysis receives greater emphasis. If the broad focus on conflict and rule-making prevails, then we can expect the orientation to contribute significantly to the formulation of public policies. If, on the other hand, microsociological attention to relevant social-psychological processes gains ascendance, then the approach probably will contribute little in the policy realm, though it may, of course, make very useful contributions to sociological theory.

In conclusion, it should be clear that the labeling approach to studying deviance and control is likely neither to undermine the legitimacy of workable, sensible, and humane rules and control

---

23 For a good general discussion of juvenile-court reform, see the recent study by Edwin M. Lemert, *Social Action and Legal Change* (Chicago: Aldine, 1970).

24 Gouldner, *The Coming Crisis of Western Sociology* (New York: Basic Books, 1970), p. 379.

processes nor to provide a panacea for the problems created by disturbing and offending behavior. It is not a revolutionary new approach to the analysis of social problems but rather a reordering of emphases in such analysis, a reordering that may help us to view deviance and control in a realistic, comprehensive, and sociologically meaningful light. It will thus continue to deserve our serious attention.

Index